Swing Trading
A Beginners And Advanced
Guide For Effective Trading
Tactics, Make More Money And
Reach Financial Freedom

D1799626

Also by Michael Branson

Swing Trading A Beginners And Advanced Guide For Effective Trading Tactics, Make More Money And Reach Financial Freedom

Introduction

Swing trading is about taking a short-term position in the market where by you identify recurring patterns in a stock price line, and then use that to your advantage to ride the wave and make a profit. It can be described best as the middle ground between the highly hectic and stressful world of day trading and the much more academic and studious approach of position trading. It can be said to be the best of both worlds as you don't have the stress of making a quick decision as you have the time to think things through. You can, for example, look at the recent data to see if you are trading on the correct side of the market, which is always a good thing. But as you also don't have the time and resources available to the position trader you do not get too caught up in your research which can lead to procrastination. Whereby the more you study a company's stock, the more confusing it becomes as you are trying to make sense of conflicting indicators which leads to analysis paralysis.

In swing trading, however, you are working on positions that last more than a day but in most likelihood less than a week, as you should focus on only one leg of a swing. That means you have the luxury of time to research and hone your strategy but not too much time to over think things.

Swing trading is, therefore, for many, a happy medium between day and position trading where you do have the opportunity to research and make informed decisions, but at the same time, you are looking for quick entry and exit points within a trade that makes you a profit on that price swing. After all, this is the core principle of swing trading; you study a trend then find a good low-price entry point, and then you ride the wave till the crest and quickly exit pocketing the profits.

Swing trading, however, is not easy, it requires that if you want to be successful that you perform diligent research and use wisely the subsequent knowledge you have discovered. This information is found through your fundamental and technical analysis – it is your analysis of the fundamentals of the company that makes you want to trade their stock, but it is the technical analysis that lets you manage and safely exit a trade. Never lose sight of the fact that wise account management and preservation of your capital is what will keep you in the game. Therefore, in this book, we strive to provide you with good advice and best practices that will enable you to build a sensible strategy that enables you to stay on the right side of the market.

With these good intentions in mind, we will give you, through the course of this book, profound advice on trading strategies, capital preservation, risk management, and position sizing. But it is not all doom and gloom because we will also show you how to identify emerging high-performing stocks and when and where to enter and exit a trade so that you optimize your profits. We will also show you how to lock-in your profits while you continue to ride the wave to even greater profits.

Swing Trading is by no means easy, but if you follow the advice in this book you will firmly have put the odds on your side, you will be confident in trading with the correct strategy in the market as well as in balancing your risk and reward dilemma - and you can't really ask for more than that.

Chapter 1: What is Swing Trading?

In this first chapter, we are going to introduce the concept of swing trading. It's essential to distinguish swing trading from other common methods of trading and investing and you also need to know what the requirements for entry are. After introducing the concept of swing trading, we will explore how swing trading differs from day trading and also how it differs from long-term or buy and hold investing. We will also explore the question of who is best suited for swing trading. Before you start, you need to know if this is something that would be good for you and your financial situation. We will do that in the chapter with a discussion of the tax implications of swing trading.

What is swing trading?

The concept of swing trading is deceptively simple. All it means is that you buy and sell stocks or other investments to make short-term profits. In other words, swing trading seeks to profit from short-term price movements on the stock market (or other markets such as currency trading). However, unlike day trading, the price movements we are interested in last from days to weeks or possibly up to a couple of months or so.

It differs from day trading in one key aspect. Swing trading involves holding securities overnight, possibly for weeks at a time. Therefore, you can be looking for short-term swings in the price of a stock, for example. However, you aren't looking for that swing in price to occur over the course of a single day, but rather over a few days, or weeks. Some people who swing trade can even lengthen that time period out to a couple of months or so. You might even say you are a swing trader if your strategy is to hold stocks for several months, but buy low and sell high over that period.

As you might guess, the level of involvement and stress in swing trading is lower than what you would find with day trading. We are going to explore the differences between swing trading and day trading in detail in a later section. Nevertheless, generally speaking, it's going to involve less upfront capital and a lower level of involvement in the daily movements of stocks or whatever market you are involved with. Swing trading can be used on stocks, Forex, commodities, and even with crypto currencies. However, for the purposes of this book, we will generally focus on the stock market. The principles are the same no matter what you trade.

Where can you use swing trading?

Swing trading can be used in virtually any market. It's a technique, rather than something specialized for a specific market like crypto currency. Nevertheless, swing traders primarily trade on stock markets. But you can use swing trading as a technique when trading commodities, currencies, and anything else that will see price swings up-and-down over the time periods of interest, and that means you could apply swing trading to anything that gets traded. You could even think of trading options as a form of swing trading since you're hoping to profit on the same moves of the stock, although options are quite a different ball game overall.

Our focus in this book is going to be on stock trading. But keep in mind that you could use the exact same techniques, including the methods of analysis for the most part on currency markets as well.

How does swing trading differ from day trading?

Firstly, let's make an observation. You cannot day trade without making it a full-time living. Starting from some first principles, a day trade is one that opens and closes the position on the same day. You might only hold the stock for a few hours or even for a matter of minutes.

From this definition, you can understand that you need to be paying strict attention to the movements of the stock or security on a moment-by-moment basis. The first thing you do with day trading is you need to know the exact right moment to buy the stock. Of course, there are high odds that you will guess wrong (not that day traders "guess"). But what's working against you is that over the short term, although traders do utilize a lot of analysis in their work, the stock market is essentially a chaotic system, with a lot of randomness built into it.

Secondly, there is the problem of what is the right moment to sell. Therefore, you are going to need to know when to get out of the position at just the right time so that you're exiting and able to make good profits. That is a very tough and nerve-racking game to play.

Of course, there are many good methods that, if followed to the letter, can produce success in day trading. That is not something anyone is going to do on the fly and be successful at. There may be that one person in a thousand that can do that, but most people are going to need extensive training. Even then, the reality is that most day traders fail to make consistent profits, or even profit at all.

With swing trading, you're looking to profit on price moves, but it's a far more relaxed method. If things are not working out for you on any given day, you can wait it out.

Another important difference between day trading and swing trading is that day trading has substantial capital requirements up front. In order to be a day trader, the vast majority of brokerages are going to require that you have $25,000 in your account. That doesn't necessarily have to be $25,000 in cash; it could be a $25,000 combination of cash and stocks. That said, it's a significant barrier to entry for many people. Even people who have $25,000 on hand may not want to risk it all on a few day trades.

There are a couple of brokerages that don't have this requirement, and they allow you to day trade with any amount of funds. However, they charge massive commissions. Those may be suitable to learn on, and you can even profit. But professional traders don't use them because of the high commissions, and you probably wouldn't want to stick with them long term if you find out you have a knack for day trading and can make profits from it.

Day trading as a defined category goes well beyond what brokerages think; it's a matter of law and even taxes. There are strict legal definitions that were created by the United States government that say exactly what a day trader is. The first part of the definition to be aware of is that you are going to be labeled a day trader if you enter into four-day trades within any five-day period. Just to be clear, a day trade is defined as buying and selling the same security on the same trading day.

Also, keep in mind the five-day period does not end at the weekend or include weekends. Therefore, it's any five consecutive business days. Alternatively, as they say in the business, five consecutive trading days.

A swing trader, in contrast, is someone that is going to hold the position at least overnight. In fact, swing traders may hold a position for several days, weeks, and even out to a few months in time. A swing trader simply holds his positions for a far longer amount of time than a day trader does.

Secondly, there are no capital requirements imposed on swing traders. If you have five dollars in your account and buy a share of a stock that is five dollars a share, you can swing trade that one share of stock. The only requirement for swing trading is that you have the capital available that you need for your own personal goals (and any requirements that your broker has to open an account, if any). Of course, buying one share of a five dollar stock isn't going to get you anywhere financially, but the point is swing trading isn't really an official designation to the point that day trading is. As far as the broker is concerned, a swing trader isn't any different from any other investor.

When you are buying a stock traditionally, as we will see in the next section, you will do so based on the fundamentals of the company. What that means, in a nutshell, is that you're going to be looking at the recent history of revenues and profits ("recent" being over the past five years), the management team, price to earnings ratio and whether or not the stock is undervalued. You would also be looking at the company's long-term prospects, as well as its history. What are the products it is coming out with? Is it engaged in R&D? Will it be expanding into new markets? Fundamentals mean looking at something for long-term investment and really getting into the business that the company is engaged in.

Day traders are not concerned with the fundamentals of a company. That could come into play at times, like on a day when a company has an earnings call. For a day trader, the concern is based on how the stock is moving over a few minutes or hours. This fact may have absolutely nothing to do with fundamentals or, as our example of an earnings call illustrates, it could be related to it. The point is: fundamentals are of prime concern for long-term investors, but it's a tangential or fleeting issue for day traders.

Day trading moves might be based on euphoria or panic of people trading at the moment. How many times have you seen the market go up or down based on a news story? Those changes are usually fleeting, but day traders seek to profit from them.

Day trades could be based on the release of a new product or some other short-term event that drives the share price up. There are many reasons and to be honest as a day trader in many cases, you don't even have to care what the reasons are. Instead, you're just looking at the charts and so forth to spot a short-term move in the stock price, either up or down. The techniques of analyzing the charts and data in the stock market to spot a possible short term move up or down and share price is called technical analysis. Long-term investors don't pay attention to that at all. As far as a long-term investor is concerned, technical analysis may not even exist. Swing traders, however, need to understand technical analysis, although they don't have to be the experts at it that day traders have to be.

So in short, a swing trader kind of takes a middle ground between the two extremes of day trading and long term investing. As a swing trader, you will be paying attention to technical analysis, but it won't take as central a role as it does in day trading. Secondly, while day traders pay relatively little attention to fundamental analysis, generally speaking, a swing trader is going to be much more interested in the fundamentals of the company. But not quite as focused as a Warren Buffett who looks at long time horizons.

Who is swing trading suitable for?

With the previous thoughts in mind, it should be clear that a day trader is going to be working on trading full-time. There really isn't an option to be a part-time day trader if you expect to make consistent profits. Of course, people might get lucky from time to time buying low and selling high on the same day, but to make consistent earnings you need to be doing live technical analysis and constantly follow financial news. It's a full-time job.

In contrast, it is possible to be a part-time swing trader. Swing trading can be suitable for people who have a full-time job they don't want to give up, and as a result, can't day trade as a practical matter. That said, swing trading is also suitable for people who actually want to do it full-time. So it's actually a more flexible approach to trading in general.

One of the differences between swing trading and day trading is that swing trading is something that can be used by people who don't have much time to devote to following the markets and financial news. That said, you still have to pay attention to those things. A passion for the stock markets in financial news and business is something that a swing trader will need.

Swing trading and day trading also carry different levels of risk, something that needs to be emphasized a lot. Let's be clear – like any trading or investment, swing trading carries risk. Overall, it's a lower risk as compared to day trading.

Let's sum it up. A day trader is somebody who's going to enter into multiple trades on the same day. At the very minimum, the day trader is going to buy and sell a security on the same day, which would be two trades. Day traders do not hold positions overnight.

The primary analysis tools used for day trading are technical tools. These will include charts, candles, and moving averages that can tell a day trader where herd behavior among traders is heading. Day trading requires an advanced understanding of technical analysis. If you aren't sure what technical analysis is, don't worry, we will be talking about it in this book.

Fundamentals can be a concern for the day trader, but not necessarily. A day trader will buy stock in a company with horrible fundamentals if they think the company is going to have a short-term rise in share price they can profit from. Alternatively, they could short the stock; something long-term buy-and-hold investors aren't interested in doing.

Remember also that a day trader must have $25,000 in his or her account, something that isn't required for anyone else. Significant losses are possible, and it's generally considered that you have a loss potential of up to 100% of your capital.

Of course, a smart trader is going to use techniques like stop-loss orders to mitigate losses, which we will talk about in this book.

Swing trading, in contrast, doesn't require a full-time commitment or the investment of large amounts of capital to get started. So you can start with small amounts of upfront money and do it on a part-time basis. Swing trading also combines fundamental and technical analysis at a far greater degree than day trading usually does. Although you won't do it to the extent that Warren Buffett would, you are going to be paying attention to the fundamentals of the companies you invest in. Think about it – is a stock going to rise over the course of a few months for a company that doesn't have some good fundamentals? Probably not.

Overall, swing trading is a far more flexible approach. You can do it part-time or full-time, with small amounts of money up front or by investing large amounts of money. You can gradually grow it over time, starting out small and working up to a larger account and engaging in larger trades as time goes on. Finally, relatively speaking, the risk is lower.

Swing trading in a nutshell

When you are engaged in swing trading, you are going to look at buying shares of stock when you believe they are at a relatively low position. This could happen for multiple reasons. For example, it could be the case that shares of stock have dropped in price because there has been a recent selloff. This happens all the time, and there are often market panics over fleeting news items or a remark that President Trump made. You should always see such downturns as a buying opportunity. Whether the markets go back up in a day or a few weeks or even months matters not to the swing trader. The one certainty is that when stocks drop because of a massive sell-off, they will go back up. The key is knowing when the best time to buy is so that you can maximize your profits later.

There could be other reasons to expect a price swing. For example, there may be an upcoming earnings report. That can be something that could go one way or the other, which means you'll have to be carefully studying the financial news to have an idea of what is going on. For example, Tesla may be about to announce that they are going to be able to ramp up production of the Model 3. This could represent a buying opportunity if you get a hold of your shares before the announcement is officially made. Therefore, you could buy shares a week or two before the announcement. Then when it is official, you can be reasonably certain that the share price is going to rise substantially. Then when it does, you sell your shares and book your profits.

Of course, there is an inherent risk – the announcement might go the other way instead, which could mean heavy losses. As we'll see, you should protect yourself with stop-loss orders to prevent massive wipeouts. However, the swing trader isn't as impacted by changes as the day trader is. Remember that you can hold your position for as long as you like. So another strategy in response to a trade that doesn't work out – provided that you are able to tie up the capital and have other capital to work with in getting into other trades – is to simply hold on and wait for other factors to cause a favorable price move.

As we mentioned in the first chapter, there isn't any official rule for time frames used in swing trading. You can enter into a trade, hoping that the price is going to move high enough to make substantial profits in a matter of days. Or it may be a week or several weeks before you end up selling your shares. It could even be six or nine months. It's entirely up to you, and it's a far more flexible way of trading than day trading.

However, one important consideration is that you're not doing your trades randomly. So you aren't going to load up on shares of a specific company and then hope they increase at some point and call that 'swing trading.' With swing trading, you are going to enter into a certain trade because you have done the analysis and believe that the share price is at a relative low, and your analysis tells you that in the coming days, weeks, or months, the share price is going to see a substantial rise.

Can you swing trade index funds?

The answer is definitely yes. Many index funds track virtually everything, from the S & P 500 to emerging markets to REITs. In this case, we are talking about exchange-traded funds. Moreover, exchange-traded fund or ETF as they are known is traded on the stock market, but it's a pooled investment like a mutual fund. You are not going to swing trade mutual funds; they have high expenses and only trade once a day, so as a swing trader it is not something you are going to be interested in at all. Nevertheless, exchange-traded funds are an entirely different ball game even though there are many similarities. For our purposes, the only things that are important about exchange-traded funds are that they trade like stocks on stock-market exchanges and that many of them are subject to wild price swings. One that may be of interest to you is SPY – an ETF that tracks the S & P 500. You can also look at DIA, an ETF that tracks the Dow Jones Industrial Average. As you know, the Dow Jones and S & P 500 can go through significant price movements based on what happens in the news. You can pay attention to things like upcoming jobs reports, GDP growth, and trade deals. Political events and terrorist attacks can also have a big influence on these indexes. That means if you are going to utilize them in your swing trading, you need to be paying close attention to financial, economic, and political news. One tweet from the President can send the markets down fast, or make them rise just as fast. So next time the President issues a tweet, keep in mind that could be a major buying opportunity for SPY or DIA.

The techniques here would be the same, even though the influences are more of general sentiment rather than paying attention to a specific stock and what a company is doing. Over time, the indexes move upwards, that is just a historical fact. But they can also swing up and down quite a bit over shorter time periods. So look for buying opportunities first, bad news that causes them to dip. Then you can buy shares and then be prepared to sell them. Your selling position may simply be a goal that is gradually reached as the stock market inevitably goes up as time passes or it might happen when good news suddenly hits, such as breaking news that GDP growth was over 3%. At that point, you unload your shares and take the profits. Of course, the next time bad news hits and the indexes crash again, that's going to be another buying opportunity.

Clear goals, limit orders, and stop-loss orders

Most people go into the stock market without having clear, specific goals in mind. They just hope to make money. That is not a successful approach for a swing trader. As a swing trader, you need to have specific, clearly delimited goals in mind. That means not letting emotions take over.

Suppose, for the sake of example, that you have purchased 1,000 shares of SPY at $288 per share. Your goal might be to make $4 per share. In the event that it drops to $286 per share, you might want to exit the position out of concern that further losses would be more than you would willingly accept and you also want to exit the position so that you could put the capital to work somewhere else.

Leaving this to fate is a bad idea. Most people place what is known as market orders on their trades. Therefore, you simply sell your shares at the prevailing market price. Doing this while swing trading is going to require that you manually take action when you reach your goals. That, of course, can be a problem because you might start getting excited over a rise in share price, having visions of dancing dollar bills as the profits come in. The risk here is that you will wait too long to exit the position, and the share price will drop wiping out even minimal profits.

That's why you need to set specific price boundaries for your buying and selling of the shares. In addition, it is better to have them automatically enforced. In the case of selling at a profit, you can place what's called a limit order. A limit order means you specify the price you're willing to accept, but the sale of the shares won't actually happen unless and until the share price reaches that level. In our example, you could place a limit order of $292 for the SPY to sell it. A limit order can be used to buy or sell a given stock at the specified price or higher. So in this example, if the share price rises to $292 or better, then your shares will be sold automatically, and the proceeds will be credited to your account.

Keep in mind that if the price doesn't go to $292 or higher, your limit order would never be executed. If you wanted to exit the trade, you could cancel the order and sell at the current market price. So maybe SPY goes to $290, and that is not as much as you hoped, but its languishing with no near term indication of an upward trend in price.

You could cancel your limit order and place a market order just to sell the shares and take the smaller level of profits.

You could also place a stop loss order, which is essentially a limit order to sell the shares if the price drops to a certain point or lower. Therefore, in this case, you could place an order to sell the shares if the price dropped to $286. If that happened, the sale would occur automatically. That would protect you from the catastrophic result of a massive sell-off that sends the share price crashing.

The 1% Rule

Financial advisors suggest that you only risk 1-2% of your account on a single trade. If you have a $50,000 account, that means only risking $500 to $1,000 on a single trade. What this does not mean is that you would only buy $500-$1,000 worth of shares; it means that you use a stop loss order to limit potential losses, and the number of losses would be limited to $500-$1,000.

As a simple example, if you limit your losses per trade to 1% on a $50,000 account, that means a maximum of a $500 loss. You can decide how much per share you are willing to lose to determine how many shares you can buy. If we decide we can lose $0.50 per share, then that would mean we could buy $500/$0.50 = 1,000 shares. Of course: you have to be able to afford the 1,000 shares. AMD is trading at $32 a share, so we could buy 1,000 shares for $32,000, and place a stop loss at $31.50 per share, which means the shares will be sold automatically if the price drops to that price point.

Of course, there are risks involved, the share price could drop to $30 a share and then rebound later to $34 a share, and since you had that stop loss in place, then you would miss out on that particular price movement.

Let's return to our example of SPY, with a potential loss of $2 per share (buying the shares at $288 per share and selling them at $286 per share with a stop loss order) then, using the 1% rule, that would enable us to purchase $500/$2 = 250 shares. Using a 2% threshold, that means we could risk $1,000/$2 = 500 shares. Unfortunately, either one entails more money than we have in our account at $288 per share, so we'll have to go with a different scenario. We could raise the possible loss per share we are willing to accept to $3 a share. This means we could buy $500/$3 = 167 shares. The cost at $288 a share would be $48,096, nearly our entire account. Nevertheless, if you are expecting big news, or you're getting in early after big news already came out, it might be worth it.

First, let us look at what happens if we lose out, and the share price ended up dipping to $285 a share. In that case, if we placed a stop-loss order, it would be executed. We'd lose $3 a share for a total of $3 x 167 = $501. The sale would generate 167 shares x $285/share = $47,595 that we would have back in our account for use with other trades. If the share price kept dropping, say to $279 a share, we would breathe a sigh of relief knowing that we had protected our principal, for the most part, taking what is really a small loss at $501. If we had waited until the shares dropped to $279, we would end up selling for $46,593, resulting in a much larger loss of capital of $1,503. You can see how a stop loss can protect you from large losses.

This is more important for swing traders, actually. As a swing trader, you might not be in front of the computer all day. If you are a part-time trader, you might be in a meeting at work when the price drops to $279 per share, or even lower. Therefore, you would have missed the opportunity to sell off the shares manually or you might be taking a shower. Things can happen fast on the stock market, and it is best to protect yourself using pre-determined boundaries that are acceptable rather than changing it. Also, note that people can have their judgment clouded when prices are dropping. If you were lucky enough to be at your computer, you might hold on at $279 a share, convincing yourself that it's got to go up soon, since it was $288 a share just a day or two ago. What happens if instead it drops to $275 a share and stays there?

On the upper end, if we bought 167 shares and the price ended up going to $293, but we sold at $292, then we'd have 167 shares x $292/share = $48,764. So we'd profit by $668.

The point of this exercise isn't to focus on the specific numbers – rather, you should focus on the mindset and actions taken. These are the mindset and actions that a successful swing trader will rely on. Always protect yourself from massive losses by using a stop loss order, and be disciplined in selling your shares and taking realizable profits rather than waiting too long, when things often decline again in nearly inevitable fashion.

Chapter 2: Tools and Platforms for Swing Trading

If you want to swing trade, you're going to need to open a brokerage account. A brokerage is just a company that plays the role of middle man. The brokerage maintains an account for you and keeps records of your trades. It also allows you to deposit funds that can be used for trading, and allows you to take out your profits. They will also take care of the necessary tax forms on your behalf. The central role of the broker is to execute trades. So when you want to buy or sell shares, the broker will do that on your behalf. You can also borrow shares from the broker, or borrow money to make larger trades, if you have a margin account.

Before choosing a broker, you're going to want to decide what financial assets you want to trade. Some brokers might not give access to all types of securities. This might be more important if you are interested in trading Forex or cryptocurrencies, finding good stock brokers is fairly straightforward. However many of the leading stockbrokers will also provide access to trading Forex, crypto, and other assets.

Types of Accounts

The first thing you're going to want to consider is whether or not you want a full service brokerage or a discount broker. A full service brokerage is one that provides professional financial advisors to help you make your investment decisions. Some may even be able to assist you with swing trading. However, be aware that commissions are going to be an important factor when you trade frequently. It's one thing to set up a periodic investment in an index fund, and quite another to be making several trades a month. For that reason, most swing traders are going to be interested in discount brokers.

Besides looking into whether or not you go with a discount broker, you are going to want to determine whether or not you open a cash account or a margin account. By law, to open a margin account you must deposit $2,000 up front. The advantage to opening a margin account is that if you qualify, it will enable you to borrow money and shares from the broker. This opens up the possibility of shorting a stock, or using leverage in order to purchase more shares than you could with your cash alone. Typically, swing traders can get 2-1 margin, which means if you deposit $2,000, you can buy $4,000 worth of stock.

Examples of popular brokerages include E Trade, Tasty works(particularly good for trading options), Robinhood (zero commissions), TD Ameritrade, along with more traditional brokers such as Fidelity or Charles Schwab. In each case, check to determine if you can trade the financial assets you are interested in trading. While its easier to have one account, if you are going to have diversified trading such as trading stocks, options, and Forex, you might have to get a different broker to manage your Forex trades. Of course it's advisable that beginning traders stick to one asset, at least at first.

Expert Advisors

Full service accounts used to only include those with a professional financial advisor. However, over the past decade or so, a new type of full service account has developed that relies on software or "robot" advisors to manage it's accounts. These often go by the name "expert advisor". This type of account is managed for you, and the robot will pick stocks/options or currency trades to buy and sell and when to sell them. That may or may not appeal to you, the idea of having a robot running your trading account might be a bit intimidating.

Retirement Accounts

Swing trading methods can be used to grow retirement accounts, such as an IRA or a 401k. However, keep in mind that you will probably be put in a position of reinvesting profits from swing trading toward the purchase of more assets inside the retirement account. So it would not be traditional swing trading in the sense of earning profits in the here and now to cash out. If you cash out early from retirement accounts, you're going to lose a lot of benefits because of heavy taxes and early withdrawal penalties.

However, swing trading is an intriguing way to grow your IRA from the inside. By law, you can only deposit about $5,000 or so per year, depending on age. But using swing trading, you have the potential to rapidly grow the account by earning profits inside of it. They can then be used to purchase more shares. If you are good at swing trading, you can double or triple the amount by which the account is growing per year, without violating any laws regarding contributions.

It's always a good idea to have a retirement account as a part of your overall portfolio, so swing trading inside the account can be part of your larger financial strategy.

Opening a Brokerage Account

Opening brokerage accounts is a pretty simple process, its like signing up for an account with anything online. Enter your name, address, and bank account information. Some brokerages may require that you make an initial deposit to get started. If you are a beginning swing trader, consider using Robinhood. This is an app based trading platform that is somewhat skeletal, but also very easy to use. With Robinhood, there are zero commissions and no minimums. So you can limit your deposits to the amount of money that you want to use for trading, rather than having to meet some arbitrary funding requirement.

Keep in mind that if you want to trade options, the broker is going to want to make sure that you understand what you are getting into. Usually, an interview of some kind is required before you can trade options. They are going to want to make sure that you understand that options are speculation and not investment. That means that you are buying financial assets in the hope that the price of the asset is going to rise over a short time period. This is in contrast to investing, where you are sinking your money into a company for the long haul. So you want to explain to the broker that you want to do speculation more than investment and that you understand what it means and what the risks are. Second, you will want to assert that you are interested in short time horizons, and not long term investing. You will also be asked some basic questions about income level and net worth. However, don't worry about those, they are pretty flexible on those points. Options trade for tens to hundreds of dollars, so you don't have to be rich to get started.

The main purpose is simply to satisfy the broker that you completely understand the nature of swing or option trading. It does not preclude you from entering into long term investments as well.

Tools Available Online

Many brokerages are self-contained, that is they include all the tools you need in order to operate as a swing trader. At a minimum, you should make sure you have access to the following:

• The ability to chart stocks out to a minimum of five years, preferably longer.

• You should be able to create candlestick charts, not just line charts.

• You should be able to easily switch between different time frames, such as days, weeks, and months.

• There should be access to moving averages, especially simple and exponential moving average tools, with the ability to set the number of periods and include more than one moving average on a chart.

• Other moving averages may be of interest, such as the Hull moving average.

• You will want to be able to utilize Bollinger bands.

• You want access to financial statements along with rundowns of cash flow.

If tools like these are not available, you can visit Yahoo Finance where they can be utilized for free. Some trading platforms have practice or simulated stock markets where you can practice trading real securities, without having to invest any money. This is a very good way to start training yourself, but of course without the strong emotions that come when real money is involved, they are of limited value.

Once you've setup your account, you're ready to get started. The next task is to learn how to analyze stocks and stock charts, and look at technical analysis.

Chapter 3: Finding A Suitable Market

In the previous chapter, we discussed swing trading techniques and how they differ from other trading styles. However financial markets have very different behaviors and some are more appropriate to swing trading than others. Therefore in this chapter, we will look at some appropriate markets in which you can as a beginner start swing trading. No bias favors a particular market; we will leave that up to you. Instead, we will try to evaluate what are and are not feasible markets for you to enter based on your initial capital.

Selecting a Financial Instrument to trade

Selecting a market in which to trade will be the first big decision you will have to make as there are several different financial markets and what they call financial instruments to choose to trade in. For instance, you can trade in shares, currency, futures, options or even crypto-currencies to name just a few. Which one you choose will depend on your interest in that field and also largely by the capital you have to trade.

The good news is that there are lots of financial instruments you can swing trade with. And each one of them has its own pros and cons. Here are some financial instruments that are considered suitable for swing trading:

Exchange-Traded Funds (ETFs): You can trade ETFs just as you would trade a regular company's stock such as Facebook (FB) or Apple Inc. (AAPL). There are ETFs for just about everything; they will track indexes and bonds, futures, commodities, stock sectors, and currencies.

Individual stocks: Possibly the most popular instrument for swing trading is trading individual company shares. There are some advantages and disadvantages to trading individual stocks compared to trading ETFs. For example, taking a position with an individual stock exposes you to the possibility of 'single event risk.' What this means is that if you are holding a long position on a trending stock, you can be vulnerable to sudden bad news. For example, if bad news about a security breach breaks, say regarding Facebook or Google, the stock can suddenly fall. However, if you were swing trading on a sector like technology that bad news might take time to affect the market. The point is that when trading individual stocks, you are always going to be vulnerable to this type of single event risk. On the other hand, typically individual stocks can outperform other companies stocks that are in the same sector such as Technology. This means that taking a position on an individual company's stock may mean that you can outperform an ETF covering the related sector.

Currencies: Forex trading is another hugely popular swing trading instrument. When trading Forex, you are comparing the relative performances of two currencies, and so you are looking for one currency to move up or down relative to the other currency. But this requires a huge amount of research into international financial markets, and it is very volatile. For example, the US dollar may go sky high or plummet compared to the Euro on the basis of a late-night tweet by a President or a CEO. Forex trading is high risk and volatile, but that also makes it attractive and if you are on the right side of the trade extremely profitable.

Cryptocurrencies: Swing trading these new cryptocurrencies has opened up a whole new market which has attracted very professional, sophisticated but also some very dubious traders and investors. The huge attraction of vast and quick profit has many amateurs entering the market which hugely inflated the realistic price. Nonetheless, the volatility of cryptocurrencies is a dream for swing traders so long as you don't get greedy.

Some of the more popular coins include, but there are many more:
- Bitcoin
- Ethereum
- Bitcoin Cash
- Ripple

Bitcoin, in particular, hit a bubble around the end of 2017 which resulted in about 80% of its value being wiped out during the 2018 backlash. Consequently, the steep price reversal led to a loss of confidence in trading cryptocurrencies, so interest has dropped significantly. But Bitcoin, in particular, has always been of interest to swing traders due to its regular periods of high price volatility for seemingly no discernible reason. Where may that put many a beginner? There are also plenty seeking potentially huge profits. As a result, Bitcoin and the other cryptocurrencies still have the potential for high price movements for swing trading.

Options: Options and Futures are a more sophisticated instrument that can be used in hedge funds and hedging positions, but they are also good for swing trading. Trading options and using them in a variety of strategies requires additional education and experience that are not quite covered here, but as a swing trader you should be aware of their existence and consider using them as you increase your knowledge.

How much Capital will I need?

This is one of the most common questions beginners ask, but there is no real satisfactory answer as it depends. The reason it depends is that the market or financial instrument you decide to trade in will largely decide what is and isn't a viable starting capital account. For example, if we take a beginner with only $1,000 of capital which must be considered as being disposable income – only trade with what you are prepared to lose – then the only viable financial instrument to trade safely is currencies using the Forex market. We say 'safely' because to avoid the risk of ruin you must only risk 1% of your capital per trade – we will explain this in detail later. Therefore, you can only in this case risk $10 per trade. Now that might not sound too bad, but we have to take the commissions and transaction costs into play. We can demonstrate this through a few examples:

If you have $1000 in your broker account, this means that you should limit yourself to $10 or 1% on each trade. But given a $1000 account size, it reduces your option to trade different financial instruments for example:

Shares

Minimum size: 100 shares

Transaction cost: $50 per round trip (buy/sell)

The transaction costs are far larger than you're allowed risk per trade. Remember you can only risk $10 per trade.

Also, the transaction costs will take a huge amount of your profits. So if you're making around 50 trades per week, you will need a return of between 150%-200% to break even.

Futures

Minimum size: 1 lot

Transaction cost: $10 per round trip

With Futures, your transaction costs eat up 1% of your return before you even start trading. And if you're making 50 trades per week, you will need a return of 50% to break even.

Forex

Minimum size: 1000 units

Transaction cost: Average 3 pips is around 30 cents

The transactions costs make trading deals on the Forex feasible as the transaction costs are small relative to your allowed risk ($10).

Therefore it might be feasible to trade Forex with a $1000 account.

But here is the problem; Forex is a volatile market and a beginner with a capital fund of $1,000 is likely to be wiped out in a matter of weeks.

There is a simple mathematical formula that can be useful when evaluating feasible instruments so that you can trade safely:

1. First, work out your risk appetite by deciding how much you are willing to lose and set the stop-loss order at an appropriate level – but keep in mind that you might not get that price as you are trying to sell when the market is not keen to buy.

2. Secondly, factor in your broker's transaction costs; this is applied to every trade

3. Add the two figures together, and if the sum is less than 1% of your current trading account, then you can consider the instrument to be feasible to trade safely.

However what is a feasible minimum capital account and what is recommended are two completely different things. For example, a capital fund of $2,000 is feasible for swing trading in shares, if the transaction rates are lower than some online broker's platform that operates with a minimum account of $1,000 and charges as little as $3.75 per transaction. However, entering the market with such small capital will restrict the number of trades that are available to you as ideally, you would want to trade the large Cap stock which is less vulnerable to market price manipulation by the market makers. Consequently, many experts recommend a starting capital account as an absolute minimum of $8,000 for trading shares.

Tools and Platforms you will need

If you are seriously entering the market, then you should do it professionally. You should consider it the way you would any other business start-up venture. Therefore you must have the capital, knowledge and the tools to do the job. The first thing you will need is an account with a licensed broker as they will do the trades on your behalf. They will also provide you with a way to make the trades typically through an online system. You should, however, shop about and try their online simulators to make sure you are comfortable with the system and the information that they give you. Fortunately, online brokers and stock trading platforms are in abundance, but your choice may be restricted by the country in which you are currently residing.

However, if you are just starting out and you do not have a trading account, then do a Google search to find a broker in your country that has good reviews.

When considering a broker look for the following things:

Account type – There are several types of accounts that are available to you as a swing trader. There will be an investment account. This style of account allows you to trade within the limits of cash deposited in the account. However, there is also an account called a Margin Account which allows you to use the money or stocks in your account as collateral so that you can borrow money from the broker. This facility of getting a loan from the broker will give you more trading power; however, you must be aware that you are now trading on borrowed money. This means you are taking on far more risk.

Transaction fees – The cost of executing a trade must be taken into account as the commission can vary greatly in price between brokers. However, for a swing trader that is just starting out the transaction fees are not quite so important. This is simply because as a beginner you should only be doing a very limited amount of small transactions a month. If not and you start out over trading then the brokers' transactions fee are likely to eat up the majority of your profit. The good news is that there are online brokers that charge as little as $3.75 per trade, but the bad news is that if you are working off a $1,000 account and sticking to the safe 1% rule, even that small commission will take most if not all of your profit.

Platforms and Tools – You want a trading system that you are comfortable with, but they vary a lot. Some online trading systems give you a lot of added features such as charts and research. Others, however, will give you the bare minimum. Also, the quality of advice and tools can vary across different brokerages. Indeed it is not just across brokerages as some firms will offer different classes of service depending on how much you're willing to pay. Nonetheless, to start out you will want a reliable online system that provides real-time quotes as well as a straight forward ordering procedure. It is also important to have a reliable system that will execute your orders immediately and also confirm your trades. That is the minimum you should be looking for, but it would be nice to have real-time charts, technical analysis tools (moving averages, support/resistance, etc.). If you are going to pay a lot for the broker's services, then you should expect research reports and opinions as well as their analysts' ratings. Fortunately finding a broker and online services is not difficult as there are many free resources and online tools available. Listed below are several excellent resources.

Finviz (finviz.com)

ChartMill (chartmill.com)

StockCharts.com (stockcharts.com)

Estimize (estimize.com)

StockTwits (stocktwits.com)

CNBC (CNBC.com)

Yahoo Finance (finance.yahoo.com)

Practice, practice, and then practice some more

Before you use your account, you need to use the broker's online simulator or start out paper trading to learn and find your risk tolerance and develop your early skills.

Traditionally the way beginners' entered the market was via an apprenticeship and spent paper trading, but today demo accounts are preferred. Nonetheless, paper trading is still an excellent way to find out if swing trading is suitable for you as it does provide valuable feedback on your trading judgment before you put your real money at risk. However, paper trading goes against the grain with many beginners to swing trading as it lacks the excitement of the real thing. Nonetheless, if you are serious about making swing trading a profitable venture then delay opening a trading account until you have practiced and believe that you are ready to start live trading.

Starting out Paper Trading

Practicing and learning the art or science behind swing trading is incredibly important. After all, what makes you think as a novice that you can just enter the market and beat the odds. The harsh reality is that you will need to practice and then learn from your mistakes. It is those defeats and your subsequent analysis that will give you the skills which will enable you to survive let alone be successful. Even if you are a skilled trader in other instruments or a hugely successful day or position trader changing codes means learning new strategies and specialized tactics. Nonetheless, as competitive as the markets are, paper trading does give you a method to practice and develop your skills. This is why and how you should do it:

• Before you, as a beginner place a live trade, you should make sure to take the time to test the waters by first trying trading out on paper. The first step is to decide the amount you want to trade. This amount will be determined ultimately by your capital and your risk appetite. But in this

• example let us keep the figures easy to work with so let's say it is $10,000

• Then you go about selecting your stock after some level of fundamental analysis you have concluded that certain stocks look to be on a promising trend wave and worth trading.

• Now what you have to do is to write on paper or notepad the current stock prices and the number of shares you want to buy with their current selling price.

• Then you must subtract the commission and transaction fees from that figure.

• Divide that trading figure by the actual share price, but remember to round down as you can't own a 1/3 or 1/2 of a share.

• Then sit back and ride the wave as you track your trades. You can easily do this by checking the closing stock price.

An example of Paper Trading To let you see how well it can work here is an example of paper trading a virtual portfolio.

In this scenario, you will start with say $20,000 and five preferred stocks. You have $4,000 per investment, but we must take commission and transaction fees into the equation, so we are less a $20 fee for buying and selling that's $9,980 apiece. Hence we are likely to buy along with this type of pattern:

Stock A: Bought 100 shares at $20 for $2000

Stock B: Bought 150 shares at $30 for $4500

Stock C: Bought 100 shares at $50 for $5000

Stock D: Bought 100 shares at $60 for $6000

Stock E: Bought 200 shares at $12 for $2400

Now what you want to keep in mind here is that the original share price isn't as significant as the percentage of price movement, i.e., the gain or loss. For example, if Stock B goes up from $4 to $34 per share. You now have $5100 in this position a profit of 11%. But the notable thing is if Stock E also goes up from $4 to $16 per share? Well, then you'd be at $3,200 in this position at a profit of 13%.

This is the thing you must remember it isn't always just about the price it is about your current position – this is determined by both the price and how much stock you hold. Paper trading is educational and can be helpful in surfacing some strange trading anomalies as well as effectively designing your own swing-trading strategy. After all, it is far better to make your mistakes on paper exercises than lose your money trading real stocks. Of course, there is a downside. It is boring, and you don't get the positive feedback that a real trade gives you – a tangible loss or gain – but you must practice and learn the skills and develop those tactics and then see whether your skills and research return a profit. An alternative approach and one many younger people favor is to use a simulator or demo account to test your skills.

Practice trading with a Demo Account

Should you find that paper trading is a bit boring, then an alternative is to use a demo account. Most brokers will give you this facility as it is a simulator that you can practice on. By all accounts, demo accounts are more enticing than paper trading as the simulators give you immediate feedback as to how your trades are performing. But of course, there is always a conflict of interest – remember they are trying to sell you a service - and you may well find that you can do no wrong. Instead, you should try out as many as you can, and practice swing trading with a wide range of tactics. At the end of the day, demo accounts are a great way to gain trading experience without losing your money. They are important to swing traders as they allow you to try out and experiment with new strategies and tactics. They also help you build confidence – but be aware some are vanity orientated - while you learn the basics of market trading.

Demos - are they realistic?

The problem with simulators and demo market games is that they are often too one dimensional. They do not sufficiently give the experience of actually losing or winning and one of the problems is they often have little context as the data is historical. But in real life, the market is based on three emotions; Greed, Fear and Hope. With the latter being the deadliest. There is no way to simulate these emotions at the depth required to represent real trading whereby you could be fabulously wealthy or wiped out in a few seconds. Instead, the best that demo accounts can do is to simulate the real trading environment without the emotions. It is not the same psychologically. Indeed physically trading with pretend money in many ways can make you learn bad habits. Nonetheless, it is an introduction to the sometimes overwhelming experience of the financial markets mayhem. Therefore realistic or not it is still a very good way to practice. There is, of course, a dilemma as most brokers provide you with these free to use demos or simulators. The problem is that they want you to play and to boost your confidence and get you to trade. After all, that's how they make their money. Hence be very wary of demos where you seem to do no wrong and especially those that reward a winning trade with a pop up acclaiming you to be a top trader.

Discovery – There is a school of thought that every trader should find their niche market by testing their skills and knowledge against different financial instruments. The belief is that it will allow you to get a feel for the market that is best suited to your temperament as markets do behave differently. An example would be that trading stocks will be different to futures or commodities.

Gain experience – Practice your techniques and strategies on paper or a demo before you risk your own money. Whatever you do practice at least entering and exiting positions, plus applying stops and limits. Also, you may want to start experimenting with short selling, but most importantly you will gain an understanding of risk and capital margin requirements, as well as in tracking your profit and loss.

Charting – The most important aspect that a beginner to trading needs to learn is how to read a chart. Even if it is just simple pattern recognition, it is invaluable in making informed decisions. Therefore you should spend time learning how to interpret price charts. What is more, you should also test your tactics and techniques against these charts to validate their effectiveness by testing the technical indicators to surface illusive patterns.

Evaluate past performance – Just about all worthy analysis is based on historical data. Machine Learning and A.I. feed almost exclusively on historical data. These clever algorithms analyze past performance data to find ways to find better solutions. They also are a good way to determine and then hone your strategy before you put your savings on the line.

Trading tools – There are a myriad of resources available to you such as the financial news, forums, and social media but how you interpret the information is the decisive factor. We all have free access to the same general information, but some make it work for them while others let it drift by. Understanding how world events can affect stocks particularly within a sector is hugely important, so pay attention to news feeds and breaking market data.

Watch-lists – As part of your overall strategy have a list of potential stock that you would like to keep an eye on. These may be stocks that you aren't sure about, but you still should keep them in mind. Many experienced traders regrets are over missed opportunities rather than bad trades so keep track of those borderline stocks.

Manage Risk– A demo account is hugely beneficial as you are betting with virtual money. Therefore gains and losses are meaningless in real terms, but they should be tactically analyzed to prevent you from repeating the mistake with your own money. Also, demos allow you to practice swing trading so that you make your early learning mistakes in a safe environment and not in the big bad world.

Price action – Demos can give you plenty of practice in reading price lines and identifying trends. One of the best ways to interpret a price line is to spot the visual patterns; however, that only comes with experience. Practicing on real price lines on a demo will give you plenty of practice interpreting those volatile movements that will allow you to profit on future real price fluctuations.

Broker and platform – Trying out a broker's online platform is a good way to evaluate their service. You can, for example, see what research and charts they provide and also see what they charge extra for. Also you can get a taste of how good they are by dipping into their forum and taking account of the sentiments of the regular poster.

Strategy

Test before you play – This is a great advantage that you as a swing trader have in your favor as it means you have time on your side. So leverage that and test before you commit to a trade. You might hear on a forum of some miracle indicator or fool-proof method to beat the market but always try it out on the demo first. Demos are a perfect place for experimentation as losses cost you nothing. Hence they are perfect for trying out new tactics or adjusting your strategy. Always test before you trade as even the best looking metrics can turn out to be rubbish when used out of context. Remember some of the greatest and successful swing traders use a combination of ten or even twenty metrics when evaluating a trade. But even they admit it can be confusing so always test a new tactic before you trade. Using a demo account will enable you to try out new things without risking losing your money. After all most trading mistakes come about due to over exuberance which leads to overtrading or through fear where profits are cut short. Another flaw is in a beginner steadfastly adhering to a directional bias, which can also be detrimental if you haven't practiced – and learned about trends and reversals -on a demo accounts beforehand.

Backward/Forward testing – Another great use for a demo account is for backward or forwards testing. The idea here is that once you have a tactic or change in strategy in mind, you can either backtest against historical data or forward test your trading plan using forecasting. While backtesting is very useful as you are working on objective data, it does tend to lack emotional excitement. On the other hand, forward testing is about projections, and this enables you to put your battle-plan into action in real-time. As a beginner however you should always stick to backward testing till you gain experience.

Drawdowns – There will be days where the market is working against you or psychologically you are just not up for the fight. However, these are the days when experimenting with new tactics on the demo account can pay dividends. You might discover a new metric that turns your trading average around or more likely see how you would be better adjusting your position size until things turn around.

Drawbacks to Demo Accounts

Now we have just spent the last few paragraphs telling you how great demo simulations are, but unfortunately, there are some downsides. Therefore before you go rushing out to get hold of a demo account on which to learn swing trading, you need to read this. Demo accounts for swing trading do have certain important limitations:

Execution – Demo accounts do not always relate to real-world conditions. This is because demo accounts are virtual, so they relate to the data at hand, so they usually fill a market order at a price offered. However, in the real world there is not always a buyer conveniently there to meet your asking price so, in a live market, there is some amount of slippage. This slippage means that some orders are not being filled immediately at the price that you wanted. Of course with falling stock, this means there are more sellers than buyers, which will make matching a deal more difficult. This makes setting loss-orders that meet actual levels of risk very challenging.

Unlimited capital – One of the strange things about online demos is that they provide you by default with vast capital to play with. Now there is a good reason for this. The reason they give you almost unlimited virtual funds is that gains are accelerated and losses can be easily recuperated if you have sufficient funds. This is what is called the risk to ruin ratio; should you bet $10 and lose the bet you will need on your next bet to cover that loss as well as get the expected gain and with limited funds this soon becomes unfeasible.

Dubious Data –Many brokers host dubious demos where you basically can do no wrong. These types of vanity sites are

deliberately enticing you to trade with them based on a false premise – that you are good.

Deposits – Although you should always be practicing using virtual money some brokers will require an initial deposit or your credit card details to use their demo accounts. If that is the case, then you should walk away.

Leverage – Many beginners get caught up in the initial winning streak on demos and seem to enjoy the irrational behavior of the system as they enjoy ever-increasing success. While this can instill confidence and result in substantial virtual profits, it does not transport well to a live-trading environment where it will almost certainly lead to significant losses.

Unfulfilled Orders – In demo accounts, everything is a virtual reality so if you trade at a price the order will be fulfilled. But in the real world things are more complex, and often there are no buyers for the stock you want to sell - at least at that price. Therefore trades in a demo always go through as executed. However, when live trading, orders will often go unfulfilled.

Trading tools – All those charts and research that you got in your demo account will suddenly come at an additional cost when you switch to live trading.

Market movements – Demo simulators are just that; simulations of the market so they do not always have real-time data, so your demo account server may not take into account up to the minute changes. These can include updates on out of hour's price movements.

Psychological effects

Emotions –The three emotions behind trading are Fear, Hope, and Greed that you may experience when you live trade. The fear of losing your capital is understandable so only trade what you can afford to lose. Greed, on the other hand, can make you ride a wave for too long. But it is hoped that is the deadliest of all. Demo accounts cannot replicate this toxic environment.

Risk Management– Complacency is another major sin, if you do not take your trades seriously, you may overlook potential unclaimed profits or overlook potential trends. However with a practice account and diligent practice these flaws can be overcome. It is a simple fact that beginner traders will be more risk tolerant trading on virtual money than they would with real cash. This maverick behavior also seems to appear when they shift to live trading.

Overtrading – The thrill of trading the seemingly endless possibility to earn free money can cause many beginners working on a demo account to overtrade. However, this can be a very bad habit as this behavior can develop into a tendency to overtrade on the live market. You need to know quantity doesn't always trump quality.

Opening a Demo Account

When you decide that swing trading is for you then look online to find a broker and open an account. Of course, bear in mind everything that we have told you about finding a suitable broker that matches your needs should be relatively straightforward. It probably is best, but that is up to individuals to go for a broker with a good online demo system. The advantage of having a good demo system is that you can play about and test out all those tactics and metrics before you go too far into real-life trading.

Testing Stop-Loss

A "stop-loss" is a fixed price order that you make against a given trade that will trigger an automatic sell when the price hits that level. This mechanism can protect you in the event of a sudden fall in price perhaps through overnight market activity.

However, a stop-loss can also be used to lock-in profits in that scenario you would sell and take the profit when the price reached a desirable high level. Some traders adjust stock-loss or profit-take levels every day. They may even adjust what they call a "trailing stop" on their current positions. They do this by setting an order to trigger at, 10% or 15% below the price they paid for the stock. Of course, this requires that you continually evaluate what 10 or 15 percent is relative to your current stock value. This means that you will have to regularly check your stock position and calculate the new stop-loss position. Once you calculate the new stop-loss level, you will need to make an order to trigger at that level. This prevents losses. However, it can work the other way and lock-in profits. For example, if you bought a stock at $10 then set a stop loss at $15 and the stock goes to $20; that is a lot of unclaimed profit should the stock plummet. But here is the thing, once the price hits $15 it would be sold giving you $5 profit per share.

However, be warned as it can have unintentional results; for example, a stop-loss applied to some stocks may well back bounce quickly. Indeed a lot of investors have found themselves in the position where they have been "stopped out" of stock overnight. Only to see it bouncing right back up the very next day and reach a tremendous high. Of course, the opposite is also true that should your stock stop-loss order trigger after a 15% slide, and the stock keeps on tumbling, then it will save you a lot of money. But you will need to know the risks as well as the rewards when applying for stop-loss orders.

There are two types of order that a trader can initiate; a market order and a limit order. A market order will strive to buy the requested amount of stock at the best market price. A limit order, on the other hand, will only buy an available stock at a designated price.

Therefore we can use these orders to fulfill different tasks such as if we issue a "limit order" which has the same mechanics as a stop-loss order but is used on the upside. For example, you may want to buy Facebook stock, but currently, it is too expensive, so you are waiting for it to drop in price. In this scenario, you could place a limit order that tells the market that you're willing to buy stock but at only this price. Moreover, you can also use limit orders when transacting a sale. For example let us say that shares in a company are currently trending downwards and trading at $290, but $300 is your break-even price. It would be good to have an order that triggers a sale at $290 to limit your losses.

Now many people will say why sell at less than you bought for? And many professional traders do set a limit order and then steadfastly refuse to budge from it. However, if you contemplate the risk, you will see that if you refuse to sell at $290, the stock could backslide to $280 or continue to plunge into deeper losses. But there is also the thing it might rebound to $300 before it breaks out and hits $500. On the buying side, if you refuse to any pay more than $10 for a stock you are not convinced about as it is currently trading low, then you too can be caught out. For you could miss the opportunity to ride the wave when it goes up to $11 and then rises to $12 and then $14 and then $15, by that time you might feel $10 was in hindsight a very good price.

Chapter 4: Problems With Swing Trading Using Options

Swing trading is one of the most common ways of trading in the stock market. Whether you know it or not, you probably have been swing trading all these while. Swing trading is buying now and then selling a few days or weeks later when prices are higher, or lower (in the case of a short). Such a price increase or decrease is known as a "Price Swing", hence the term "Swing Trading".

Most beginners to options trading take up options as a form of leverage for their swing trading. They want to buy call options when prices are low and then quickly sell them a few days or weeks later for a leveraged gain. Vice versa true for put options. However, many such beginners quickly found out the hard way that in options swing trading, they could still make a substantial loss even if the stock eventually did move in the direction that they predicted.

How is that so? What are some problems associated with swing trading using options that they failed to take note of?

Indeed, even though options can be used quite simply as leveraged substitution for trading the underlying stock, there are a few things about options that most beginners fail to take note of.

Strike Price

It doesn't take long for anyone to realize that there are many options available across many strike prices for all optionable stocks. The obvious choice that beginners commonly make is to buy the "cheap" out of the money options for higher leverage. Out of the money options are options that have no built in value in them. These are call options with strike prices higher than the prevailing stock price or put options with strike prices lower than the prevailing stock price.

The problem with buying out of the money options in swing trading is that even if the underlying stock move in the direction of your prediction (upwards for buying call options and downwards for buying put options), you could still lose ALL your money if the stock did not exceed the strike price of the options you bought! That's right, this is known as to "Expire Out of The Money" which makes all the options you bought worthless. This is also how most beginners lose all their money in options trading.

In general, the more out of the money the options are, the higher the leverage and the higher the risk that those options will expire worthless, losing you all the money put into them. The more in the money the options are, the lower more expensive they are due to the value built into them, the lower the leverage becomes but the lower the risk of expiring worthless. You need to take the expected magnitude of the move and the amount of risk you can take into consideration when deciding which strike price to buy for swing trading with options. If you expect a big move, out of the money options would of course give you tremendous rewards but if the move fails to exceed the strike price of those options by expiration, a nasty awakening awaits.

Expiration Date

Unlike swing trading with stocks which you can hold on to perpetually when things go wrong, options have a definite expiration date. This means that if you are wrong, you will very quickly lose money when expiration arrives without the benefit of being able to hold on to the position and wait for a return or dividend.

Swing trading with options is fighting against time. The faster the stock moves, the surer you are of profit. Good news is, all optionable stocks have options across many expiration months as well. Nearer month options are cheaper and further month options are more expensive. As such, if you are confident that the underlying stock is going to move quickly, you could trade with nearer expiration month options or what is called "Front Month Options", which are cheaper and therefore have a higher leverage. If you wish to give more time for the stock to move, you could choose a further expiration month which will of course be more expensive and therefore have a much lower leverage.

As such, the choice of expiration month for swing trading with options is largely a choice between leverage and time. Take note that you can sell profitable options way before their expiration dates. As such, most swing traders go for options with 2 to 3 months left to expiration at least.

Extrinsic Value

Extrinsic value, or commonly known as "premium", is the part of the price of an option which goes away completely when expiration arrives. This is why out of the money options that is mentioned above expires worthless by expiration. Because their entire price consists only of Extrinsic Value and no built-in value (intrinsic value).

The thing about extrinsic value is that it erodes under two conditions; By time and by Volatility crunch. Eroding or extrinsic value over time as expiration approaches is known as "Time Decay". The longer you hold an option that is not profitable, the cheaper the option becomes and eventually it could become worthless. This is why swing trading with options is a race against time. The faster the stock you pick moves, the surer of profit you are. It is unlike swing trading with the stock itself where you make a profit as long as it moves eventually, no matter how long it takes.

Eroding of extrinsic value when the "excitement" or "anticipation" on the stock drops is known as a "Volatility Crunch". When a stock is expected to make a significant move by a definite time in the future like an earnings release or court verdict, implied volatility builds up and options on that stock becomes more and more expensive. The extra cost built up through anticipation of such events erodes completely once the event is announced and hits the wires. This is what volatility crunch is all about and why a lot of beginners to options trading attempting to swing trade a stock through its earnings release lose money. Yes, the extrinsic value erosion by volatility crunch can be so high that even if the stock did move powerfully in the predicted direction, you may not make any profit as the price move has been priced into the extrinsic value itself.

As such, when swing trading with options, you need to consider a more complex strategy when speculating on high volatility stocks or events and be able to choose stocks that move before the effects of time decay takes a big mouth full of that profit away.

Bid -Ask Spread

The bid ask spread of options can be significantly larger than the bid ask spread of their underlying stock if the options are not heavily traded. A large bid ask spread introduces a huge upfront loss to the position especially for cheap out of the money options, putting you into a significant loss right from the start. As such, it is imperative in options trading to trade options with a tight bid ask spread in order to ensure liquidity and a small upfront loss.

Swing trading with options can be an extremely rewarding and profitable venture when you take all of the above issues into mind and choose your options wisely.

Should I Be A Swing Trader?

Do you want to play the stock market but feel it is just too intense for you? Or maybe you have a full-time job during the day and can't sit at your computer with a direct-access system ready with your finger on mouse button waiting to click. You need a trading style that doesn't leave you bound by your stocks and hanging around for the end of the trading day. What you need to look into is swing trading stocks to fit your situation and still allow the same excitement a trader can get from making those good trades.

Swing trading is a diverse style that is popular for many reasons. This trading style relies on strong uptrends or downtrends that allow the trader to swing on a chosen trend as long as it lasts. Swing traders base their stock trading decision on a lot of research done in between working and other daily responsibilities. So, swing trading stocks has the flexibility someone needs in a stock trading style. The research is needed for a deeper understanding of the stocks one is interested in invest in.

The stock research to be done is looking back at past trends allowing you to come up with an informed decision on what to do. That way you can take a calculated risk of how long the trend will last in an uptrend or how short you need to go on a downtrend to maximize your profits. The use of end-of-the-day charts software and the information provided by your broker is also used to make your stock trading decisions. This eliminates the need of a direct-access system, being bound by your stocks and waiting for the end of the day trading.

Most swing traders generally trade in blocks of 1000 shares at a time but this is more of a guideline then a rule. In addition, these traders will hold only 10 positions at a time. The type of stocks a swing trader will choose for their stock picks are those that can be moved quickly or at least in the near future. Below is a list of criteria used by the swing trader to analyze the stocks and decide on the stock pics.

Volume and Liquidity

Wanting stocks, they can move quickly they work with actively traded and large stocks that are easier to trade.

Trending

This is the uptrend and downtrend mentioned previously. Stocks that are following these trend patterns rather than a straight one is what swing traders are looking for.

Volatility

Volatility of a stock is showing it has a lot of movement. Another criterion a swing trader looks for because the traders can profit quickly with a volatile stock.

Sector Selection

When stocks are in the strong sector the swing trader finds it easier to trade but in the weak sector profits are made by shorting a stock or the weakening price.

Tight Spreads

Tight spreads mean small spreads in the bid and the ask of a stock. Swing traders want the smaller spread because they can profit more from it. With a wider spread a trader looks to have lower profits. So, the tighter the better.

Swing trading stocks is a diverse style of trading and fits well for anyone who has a full-time job and still wants to trade. It still involves a lot of work but at least it is more flexible to do your trading with. You just have to find the time to do the research needed for swing trading stock and you will be able to feel the excitement other traders feel after making a good trade.

Thrill Of Swing Trading

Swing trading is basically a kind of stock trading. But the skill it requires is somewhat different from the normal methods. A well-disciplined approach towards the day to day happenings in each market is very necessary for a good swing trader because it is not a case where we can check for a chance, as we are putting the real money in it.

If you are not capable of taking risks then swing trading won't be a good option for you. It is true that low reward low risk trading will be very safe way. But in the swing trading with increased risk you can get good reward. The basic decision a swing trader should take is that about when to enter and quit the market for making profit. For this they cannot have any exact method or scientific way.

The swing trading strategy consists mainly of two activities buying and selling of options, stocks, bonds, currencies, commodities etc. but the process is getting complicated by considering the fact when should buy and sell these things. Swing traders can't fix a right time for the high profit through these accurate selling and buying timings. The aim should be to buy at the low prices and sell at the high price timings.

Swing trading is highly dependent on the matured behavior in the market. Swing traders are making profit or loss from the right or wrong decisions of other firms. If you can take advantage out of the wrong timings of the other traders you can make high profit by acting at the correct point. But you should be patient enough to wait for the apt timings without making hurry some decisions. But sometimes much quickness will be needed to take advantage of the situation.

Taking the wise decision at accurate time is very important. Swing trading is not about the moving with herds. One's loss is others gain. So, the self-discipline, patience and analyzing capacity will be the favorable factors in this. Aim at maximizing the profit and minimizing the loss to the portfolios.

Another fact about swing trading is that the stock will be buying at the beginning of a trending stock and holding it. Then towards the end of this trend the stock should be sold. So, the trading is basically according to the change in trends. The time period of this strategic movement may last from one week to a month. It will solely depend upon the trend and the swing trader. The experience will help the swing traders to set their timings more logically and accurately. Any way this will be a short period process.

As planning is very important in swing trading the traders will usually take the help of the history of the companies before entering in to deals. As this is a short term process the buying and selling of stocks should be very quick. For this the swing traders will prefer the stocks of heavy trading reputed companies in the market. So, it will make the entry and exit much quicker. They will make the purchases at the beginning of the boom of the particular stock then try to sell it before its returns to lower levels.

Before entering the swing trading, be confident of yourself, then make the best experience in stock trading. This will gain you a lot from the swing trading strategies. Set your plans and do a well-disciplined stock market trading.

Swing Trading Tips

Swing trading is one of trading styles which commonly implemented in speculative activity in financial markets such as bonds, commodity, foreign exchange, stock and stock index. Usually this trading style requires a swing trader to hold his or her trading position more than one trading day, commonly 2 to 5 trading days. Swing trading is popular in trading world as this trading styles usually has a good risk and reward ratio, it means the probability to gain profit is bigger than the risk that may rise in each trade.

In general, swing trading aims for 100 pips profit probability. Profit potential can be gained from every market swing. A swing trader, especially in foreign exchange and stock index market, can go both long or short to take every opportunity. It also means, within a trading week, when a market is volatile, a swing trader may come across several trading opportunities he or she can take.

Compared to scalping trading or day trading, obviously swing trading has fewer trading opportunities, however, as you can see here if you implement this trading style, probably you will have more time to do your other activities as you do not have to keep your eyes on a market all the trading day. Of course, you will only get fewer opportunities but with high probability to win for each opportunity. It is your call to choose which trading style to apply. No trading style is perfect, there is always plus and minus.

Now, if you certainly want to give a try to swing trading, you can find some strategies from many resources available in the internet. You may find some books and any other educational materials on swing trading. You can visit and be a member of some trading forums as well. However, is that there are also some fraudulent people claiming themselves as swing trading gurus but actually they just want you to buy their rubbish education materials. Just be careful to such people.

Fortunately, after getting some basic understanding and experience on swing trading, you can be a good swing trader as well. You can even come up with your own swing trading strategies. Many people enjoy the benefit of developing their own swing trading strategies as they are the only ones who know their trading character, need and style. Never quit to learn to be a good swing trader, although without a doubt it will take longer time to master swing trading excellently but in the end all of your efforts will pay out.

Chapter 5: Fundamental Analysis

Fundamental analysis is a process by which you study the fundamentals behind a financial asset. On the Forex markets, you will be looking at the state of the economy, GDP growth, and political factors that impact the overall picture and stability of the country. If these items are looking good, that means the currency for that country will gain strength. But since currencies are traded in pairs on Forex, that means you also have to compare fundamentals between countries. If Europe looks strong but Japan is looking even better, then the Japanese Yen would strengthen as compared to the Euro.

When it comes to stocks and options, the fundamentals include profit margins, price to earnings ratios, cash flow and other indicators that give a picture of the overall health and prospects of the company. You'll be wanting to take a look at quarterly earnings, and reviewing earnings calls for companies that you are invested in. Fundamental analysis also means looking for stocks that are currently undervalued. The price of undervalued stocks is likely to increase at some point in the future, so spotting an undervalued stock could be useful for the swing trader.

Since swing traders have different time horizons as compared to buy and hold investors, short-term results like earnings calls are going to take on a larger role, as compared to looking at trends in revenue and profits over the course of years. A good earnings call can send prices soaring, while failing to meet expectations can send stocks into a rapid decline. When there are events like this as a swing trader you have to be ready to seize upon them as quickly as possible.

It's also important to keep your eye on company news of a more general nature. If a product fails or ends up creating legal trouble for a company that can be an opportunity to short the stock or invest in put options. Alternatively, the release of a new product that exceeds expectations can be an opportunity to go long on the stock.

Financial Reports to Read and Where to Get The Information

The SEC requires that all publicly traded companies make audited financial statements available. This includes a prospectus and an important report filed annually which is called the 10K. In these documents you'll find audited records that include items such as cash flow, balance sheets, and other financial data. They also include important information about the management team and competition the company is facing in its sector. The company must also give shareholders an overview of its future plans and information about attempts to enter new markets. You can visit company websites to get these reports, or do an online search using the company name with "10K" or "prospectus". Summaries of financial information are also available on many stock websites free of charge. For example, you can get income statements, balance sheets and cash flow on Yahoo Finance for any company that is listed on the stock exchanges.

There is also another important report that may be released from time to time, called an 8K. These contain information similar to that found in a 10K, but they are only filed when important short term information has to be disclosed to investors. At times, the information contained in an 8K can have a major impact on share price.

Financial Statements in More Detail

There are three general types of financial statements, in case you aren't fully aware. These include the following:

• Income statement: An income statement will include information such as revenue, gross profit, and operating expenses. These reports can help you determine the overall health of the company, and you can look for trends in revenues and profits over the past few years. Be sure to look for net income as a percentage of revenue. As a swing trader, while you are going to want to have an understanding of the overall health of the company, you are going to be more interested in looking at quarterly statements and keeping up with earnings calls and other announcements.

• Balance sheet: A balance sheet shows current assets and liabilities for the company. Current liabilities are of particular note on a balance sheet. You want to look at a balance sheet thinking about the financial health of the company. Is it carrying a large amount of debt? Is the amount of debt increasing, and could that prevent the company from being profitable or paying dividends at current levels? These factors may make a company less appealing to investors. When a company is younger and in an aggressive growth phase, investors may be more tolerant.

• Cash Flow: Cash flow is a summary of items such as net income, changes to inventory, depreciation, changes to liabilities and financing opportunities among others. Cash flow can give you a good overview of recent company performance and is another way to gauge the health of the company. Pay special attention to changes in inventory. Ask yourself if it looks like the company is able to move its product.

When examining quarterly data, you'll want to compare quarterly results to the same quarter a year earlier. In many cases, company performance will depend on time of year, so the best way to see trends in the company's performance is to make an apples to apples comparison, rather than just looking at how revenue and net income changed from last quarter to the most recent quarter.

Earnings Calls

On a quarterly basis, one of the most important events for a swing trader is the earnings call of the companies that the trader is interested in. Earnings calls can lead to dramatic swings in stock price, depending on whether it's a good earnings call or a bad earnings call. In the crazy world of Wall Street, an earnings call largely depends on what people are expecting out of it, rather than any absolute measure of performance. For example, if investors expect earnings to increase 25%, and the company reports that it only grew earnings by 10%, even though any rational person would view that as a positive, Wall Street is probably going to react negatively. Of course, if the report shows a decline it's going to be that much worse. The thing about this for the swing trader is we don't know how strongly the market will react. If share price is $200, it might drop to $180, or it might drop to $170. Nobody knows ahead of time, but you should be ready to enter into your trades accordingly.

Things work just as well the other way around. If analysts were expecting a company to see a 10% increase, but they report an 18% or 25% increase in year over year profits instead, this will send the stock soaring. Again, nobody is sure how high it will go. You will have to have a preset value of profit you are willing to accept on a trade, and place a limit order ahead of time. Then you have to live with the results. If your limit order is at $220 a share, you can be happy with your $20 a share gain, even if the stock keeps rising. A disciplined trader that doesn't get greedy is far more likely to succeed over the long-term.

While it's impossible to know ahead of time how an earnings call is going to go, you can gain some familiarity with a company and how the market reacts to it by going over previous earnings calls. Do so by not only reviewing the content of the calls, but by looking to see how strongly the market reacted to them.

Keep in mind that a bad earnings report isn't just an opportunity to short stock or invest in put options. When the stock drops, it's also an opportunity to get in at relatively low price point. Don't set perfection as a goal for your trades. The only thing you should worry about is getting in on the stock when prices are relatively low as compared to the previous price level. If it continues going lower, beating yourself up over missing the opportunity is a waste of energy. Instead, focus on waiting – for the stock to go back up so you can profit at a future date.

If the earnings report turns out to be a good one, you might want to be ready to enter into your position immediately. Then you can ride the wave of rising share prices. It's not necessary to invest before an earnings call and it could even be a bad decision to do so, because you won't know for sure which way things are going to go. In any case, earnings reports are an important part of your fundamental analysis to see how the company is performing.

Price to earnings ratio

An important metric that matches share price and earnings per share is the price to earnings ratio. Investors and traders are on the look out for price to earnings ratios that are excessively high, and also for price to earnings ratios that are low in comparison to similar companies in the same sector. If the price to earnings ratio is excessive when compared to other companies in the same sector, that could mean the stock is overvalued, and might head into a downturn at some point. Conversely, an undervalued stock as indicated by a relatively low price to earnings ratio is a stock that is available at a "discount", because it's undervalued. At some point – the thinking goes – the stock is going to rise in price up to it's true value.

You shouldn't just take the price to earnings ratio at face value. If you notice one that is out of line with the rest of the industry, you should do some research to find out if there is some external reason behind the difference. That may require a detailed check of news about the company on financial websites, as well as reading press releases and 8K reports issued by the company.

An interesting and recent example is Ford Motor Company. At nearly 14, the price to earnings ratio of Ford is nearly twice that of other auto companies. Compared to GM, it's actually more than twice as big. At the time of writing, it alone stands out in the automobile sector, where all the other companies are in a similar range. It's extremely unlikely that Ford represents the standard of the sector and all the rest of the companies are undervalued.

That could mean one of two things – Ford is in for a correction at some point in the future, or Ford has recently made some moves or announcements that make it deserve the high ratio. The first step you should take is to look over financial reports and compare profit margins between the different auto companies. You'll also want to look for any news you can find about Ford in recent months.

It could be something as simple as a stock split. When a company splits its shares, the amount of money invested in the company stays the same but the number of shares changes. Splits can work in both directions. Companies can use splits to inflate or deflate price to earnings or earnings per share ratios.

In general, if the price to earnings ratio appears excessively high or low, this can indicate that the stock is in for a correction in the coming months. If it's excessively high this is an overvalued stock, and the price of the stock might be set to drop in the coming weeks. We would expect it to drop until it reaches a more appropriate level for its sector. On the other hand if its low and the company fundamentals look good, that can be a sign that the company is poised for gains. So the price to earnings ratio can indicate that an individual stock is set to undergo a "correction".

But keep in mind that there is no "right" or "wrong" price to earnings ratio. As we explained above, you will have to look at companies in the same sector to get an idea of how a given company compares to it's competitors. Obviously you don't want to compare a bank to an auto company or to a social media company. Also make sure you are really comparing the same measurement. A good one to look at is TTM. This means trailing twelve months. You will also see past-looking and forward-looking price to earnings ratios. I prefer to avoid forward looking and stick to the TTM value. To get a feel of how different they are from sector to sector, since we've already looked at automobile companies, let's compare that to some other industries.

Let's look at a younger and growing sector, social media companies. Looking at Twitter, we find that the P/E (TTM) ratio is 20.61. This is actually considered a pretty average price to earnings ratio. Looking at Facebook, the price to earnings ratio is a bit higher, checking in at 28.58. That's almost 42% higher than Twitter, but given the more successful financials that Facebook has, it's probably justified.

Now let's look at a newer company, such as SNAP. In this case, there isn't any price to earnings ratio given. That means SNAP is not profitable. Since it's a young and growing company, that's not really relevant, at least not yet. Investors are going to want to see results at some point – but for now they are relatively patient. Tesla is another example of a relatively young company that is poised for rapid growth – it has yet to have positive earnings.

Searching for some more social media companies, we find one that is way out of whack. YELP is sometimes considered a social media company, and its P/E ratio is 49.89. This is much higher than what we've seen so far. YELP is a popular website to be sure, but it doesn't seem to have any fundamentals to justify a price to earnings ratio that high. That could mean it's in for a price correction in the coming months.

We can also find examples on the other extreme. Weibo corporation has a P/E ratio of 15, which is comparably low.

You can also look at closely related companies that are similar, but not necessarily in the same exact sector. Microsoft is a technology company and they own Linked-In, so that seems like a good candidate. Their P/E ratio is 30 – about the same as Facebook.

With these values in mind, Weibo might be a hidden opportunity. Before deciding, however, you'd want to look at the company financials and read what analysts are saying about it. Something a swing trader should always keep in mind is that looking at a single metric should not drive your decision making. You need to find confirmation elsewhere.

The point of looking at price to earnings ratio is that it's a starting point for further research.

Social media is a new and growing sector. It's interesting to look at another more slowly moving sector such as banking. Here is what we find:

- Wells Fargo: 10.24
- Bank of America: 10.4
- Citigroup: 9.81
- JP Morgan Chase: 11.72

Notice how they are all clustered around the same value. If you are looking at stocks in the banking sector, any stock that had a price to earnings ratio that fell outside of the range 9-11 would be very suspect, possibly representing an opportunity to look at for a future price swing.

Open Interest, Volume, Short interest and Put to Call Ratios

Looking at options, open interest, volume and short interest are some of the factors to consider. These can also help you determine where traders expect prices to go. There aren't absolute numbers that can be used as a guideline, everything is relative.

Open interest tells you the number of options contracts for a given strike price and expiration date. Options traders seek out a minimum of 100, because this indicates enough liquidity that you can quickly get out of a trade. When you find strike prices with higher levels of open interest, these are probably price levels where expert traders are expecting the stock to go in the near future. You will want to compare open interest numbers for calls and puts on the stock. Calls are bets that the stock is going to rise in price, while puts are bets that the stock is going to decline in price.

Volume tells you the number of trades that happened on the most recent trading day. This also gives you an indication of the level of interest in the strike price – where people thing the stock price may be heading.

You can also take a look at short interest, and also the put to call ratio for options related to a stock. Short interest tells you how many investors are shorting the stock. If this number is high, that indicates that the investing community is expecting a stock price to decline in the near future.

This information is also communicated by the put to call ratio for options related to the stock. Investors who think that a stock price is going to decline are going to invest in put options. If the put to call ratio is excessive, then that can reflect an expectation of coming price declines in the stock. You can compare the value you find for a given company to similar companies in the same sector. It's also good to check the put to call ratios for SPY, which tracks the S & P 500, for a rough comparison. That will give you an indication of what investors are expecting for the market as a whole. Note that options all have different strike prices, so you will want to check the put to call ratios for different strike prices.

Futures and after hours trading

You can look at futures and after-hours trading to see how a stock is moving as a leading indicator, that might help you decide when to enter or exit a position. For futures, S & P 500 and other index futures can indicate the overall direction of the market. For individual stocks you might look at after hours trading especially after a late earnings report. This can help you determine when to enter your next trade.

Fundamental Analysis for Forex

Fundamental analysis can also play an important role for Forex traders, especially if you are holding your positions for longer periods. The types of fundamental analysis you are going to use will primarily revolve around macroeconomic factors, political factors, and trade. You are going to want to keep a close eye on GDP growth, jobs and unemployment, and trade issues that can impact currencies. Political factors at home and abroad can also weaken or strengthen a currency.

As we stated in the introductory remarks for the chapter, the strength of any given currency can't be decided in isolation. Rather, you need to look for relative comparisons. You'll also want to study past relationships between currencies to understand how they have changed historically in response to changing circumstances. The U.S. economy always looms large, but Japan and Europe are important too.

Chapter 6: Learning the Art of Swing Trading

In this chapter, we will show you how to best enter into swing trading. It is very easy, but that is where most beginners fail. Therefore if you do not want to be among the long list of failed hobbyist traders then make sure you know what you are doing before you risk your money. We will provide you with good advice on a safe starting point that will help you preserve your capital. We will show you how to hone your trading skills using a variety of techniques to get on the right side of the market before you risk your money.

Learning the Art or Science of Swing Trading

Now that you have decided to try out swing trading you will be glad to know that you can find your feet and learn the basic skills by using simulation trades based on live, real-world stock but using virtual money. Many brokerages offer this service where you can safely learn in a virtual environment. The importance of using these simulations to learn, develop and practice your trading strategies cannot be overemphasized. You will however also need to undoubtedly develop your own trading strategy that suits your pocket and risk profile. After all, you don't want to be starting out trading using real money and no tested strategy. Therefore you will need first to learn how to swing trade and practice using the simulators to hone your skills and develop a strategy. A good way to develop those strategies and skills is to follow the methodologies of experienced swing traders and copy their typical approach to swing trading.

A day in the life of a Swing Trader

What you need to do before the Market opens is essential if you want to be successful. Professional swing trader will often rise and begin working long before the start of trading. Indeed it is often as early as 6.00 am if they can sleep through their trade notifications chiming on their phones. This is because it is very important for a trader to get an early impression of the prevailing conditions that have overnight affected slant of the day's market. Diligent traders will also need to check their existing positions' profitability and the effects on them from overnight trading which can be considerable. They will need to be on the look-out for new potential trades, and they may do this by making up a daily watch list.

Get an early impression of the Market

After you shake the sleep from your eyes and get some coffee the next task of the day is to fire up the computer and get an early impression of the market conditions. The most effective way to do this for beginners that are new to swing trading is via CNBC. There are also other media channels and websites as well as subscription services. However, most professionals are not interested in the actual details they just want to know what is better or worse about something such as is the SP500 up or down, or is the dollar trading higher than the Japanese yen? They don't get too embroiled in the detail they just want to know what is better today than yesterday or worse. The beginner should take that as a good tip. You should also keep to the traditional media sources before committing to a long term subscription service. Regardless of the source of the market intelligence, the beginner trader will have to keep an eye on three specific pointers:

1. The prevalent financial market condition, whether the market is bullish or bearish

2. Stock Sector Confidence, (what sectors are hot, what sectors are growing, what sectors are cold, etc.)

3. Current Economic Climate (based on the news on the economy, GDP earnings, Unemployment, etc.)

This crucial financial information can be determined via key economic reports as well as through published currency rates and inflation figures. Though that level of scrutiny is more for the professional analysts typically the beginners can get by just through scrutinizing the general trends in the key financial markets they will trade on. Remember that many professionals only judge news based on whether it is good or bad news they are not interested in the details. For example; are the stocks in their trading category or sector up or down?

Find Potential Trade Opportunities

Traders will always be on the look-out in the morning for new potential high-value trades. Typically, swing traders will first identify and buy stock with what is known as a fundamental catalyst. The experts will then manage or sell the stock on the basis of technical analysis. Now to understand what a fundamental catalyst is and how to find good fundamental catalysts we can use one of three methods:

1. Specialist opportunities: These are the opportunities that arise from unpredictable changes in a company's standing include going public, loss of a CEO, takeovers, mergers, and other similar major events that will be reported in the financial and business orientated media. These types of opportunities will indicate high risk and are not for the

2. beginner, well at least not without considerable simulated and paper trading experience. Nonetheless, for the

3. professionals, they often deliver large profits for those who have diligently researched each opportunity.

4. Focusing on a Specific Sector: Discovering this type of high performing stock is done by studying the business news and focusing on the updates that are relative to that sectors financial news. The objective of doing this fundamental analysis is that it gives you knowledge of which sectors are performing well. An interesting thing for you to note is that individual companies within a sector such as technology will perform alike as there are a lot of synergies. They will vary obviously in price index movement, but the trends will tend to be uniform across the entire sector. For example, you will be able to

tell that the technology sector is trading hot by simply checking on the sector performance. This can be done by simply reading the news for mentions of the stock movement of the technology giants within the sector. If those giants are doing well and their stock is trending up, it is highly likely that all the other companies in that sector are undergoing a similar upward trend. Sector play will encourage the swing trader to buy into the sector sentiment rather than into an individual company's stock. That way they are free from the risk of one single company

5. having at an ill-opportune moment and then they can ride the wave of the group's strength until the trend ultimately shows the signs of reversal or retracement.

6. Chart analysis or basic pattern recognition is also another method available to swing traders. Typically this sort of information is only available for heavily traded stocks. However, these types of plays require a trader to identify an entry point into the trade. However, if they are sufficiently talented and well informed, they can identify the breakouts which involve, buying after a drop in price and then selling again at the next peak level.

Draw up a Watch List

For you as a beginner swing trader to keep on top of your research and opportunities, you are best to take another leaf out of the professional's book and create a watch list. This is a list of potentially high-performing stocks that are trading which has caught your interest. Typically these will be a list of stocks that you have been advised on or have yourself detected by some basic fundamental analysis. These stocks will look like having the potential of being a good trade. A more detailed watch list which a professional might make up each day will typically contain a list of stocks with their entry prices and stop-loss prices that they want to keep an eye on.

Calculating the Existing Positions

Most importantly you must check up on the existing positions of your stock but do it on a regular basis not sporadically. The problem with random checks is that you can see losses or gains and then trade reactively trying to chase the losses. To do this, you will first need to check your current position then if everything is stable look to the overnight financial news to ensure that nothing untoward has happened, that may affect your stocks positions. This can easily be done by entering the assigned stock symbol into Google. If there is a significant change to your position, then you will have to see how it may affect your current trading strategy. Even if it doesn't, you may want to reconsider where to adjust your stop-loss or where to set your take-profit points.

After-Hours Market

Aftermarket hours is a dangerous time as it is the time when the rest of the world is trading. But it is the time where you can watch what is going on in real time, and if you can't sleep, you may want to do some of your own tradings. But even if you do not want to trade you may want to make adjustments to your position based on global market movements that offer opportunities for future trading. However, you only want to adjust profit-taking levels or adjust stop-loss levels upward to lock in profits. It is never a good idea to increase risk by moving a stop-loss down. After all, as we will see later, risk management is critical to long-term sustainability and financial survival. This period is for the swing trader the time for performance evaluation and a time to evaluate their position. Diligently evaluating your performance over a few days involves examining your analyzing of your trading activity and seeing where you went wrong or where you were successful and then determining the areas that need some improvement. By following this typical daily routine of an experienced swing trader, the one thing that stands out is just how important it is to follow a pre-market routine diligently. The researched and analysis performed on the previous day's trading and the intelligence gathered is critical to successful swing trading. After all, you have the advantage of holding a position for several days so this time should be spent finding trading opportunities and planning the day's trading strategy. Nonetheless, the market hours are the time spent trading except for adjusting risk or profit taking positions. Certainly, they should not be used for reactively devising any new strategies. Aftermarket time should be a time to review your short term trades and assess their overall performance. By creating and following a daily trading routine this will improve your trading; also it only requires some dedication and planning and really when we consider how much of your money is at stake is that so difficult.

Chapter 7: Technical Analysis

One of the most important toolboxes for the swing trader is technical analysis. You don't have to become as much of an expert at it as a day trader would have to, but it's still very important to understand the basics and pick 2-3 tools to use in analysis to determine what trades to enter, what profit levels to shoot for, and what stop losses you should put in place to protect yourself. Technical analysis can put off a lot of people, but you aren't going to need to do any fancy math, everything is done for you, so all you need is a little bit of understanding of graphs and charts. Most of it is common sense, and you'll be looking for some transitions in your data. With swing trading, the number one error is not looking at the right time frames. You always need to keep your time frame in mind and remember that not all swing traders use the same time frames – so you need to focus on what is appropriate for your personal situation.

Moving Averages

Everyone understands the concept of an average. For the stock market, to get the average price, you simply add up the prices and then divide by the number of points. A moving average means that at each data point, you calculate the average from that data point backward for the number of time steps you want to use. So if we were using a daily stock chart, a 7-day moving average would calculate the average for the past 7 days at each point, and build up a curve using that data. The reason you want to do this is to smooth out the data into a nice curve, and that is going to give you a better idea of the trend in prices since it weeds out all the noise.

One downside about the moving average is that it's a lagging indicator. That means it's based on past pricing data. Obviously, we can't use a tool that gives us future pricing data. We don't know what that information is. Even so, moving averages give us surprising information that can be useful.

Moving averages used in the stock market analysis are either simple or exponential. What we described above is a simple moving average that is you just add up the number of data points you want and divide by the count.

So if the price of a stock was $12, $14, $10, $12, and $13 over the past five days, the moving average on the fifth day would be:

MA = $(12+14+10+12+13)/5 = $12.20

If the following day the price is $14.25, the next moving average is:

MA = $(14+10+12+13+14.25)/5 = $12.65

On the stock chart, the value of the MA would be plotted at each point and the values connected into a smooth line. The purple line in this chart shows the 50 days moving average curve for AMD, plotted along with its actual share price.

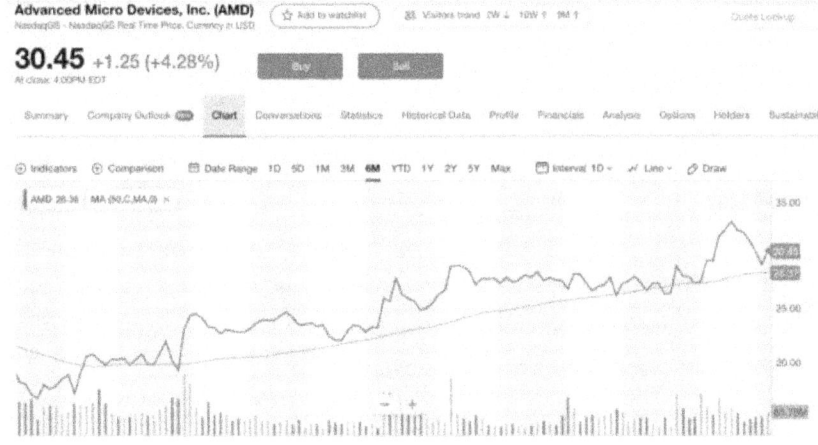

When you add a moving average to a chart, you can select the period and determine whether it uses closing price, open price, high, low, and several other options. Most of the time we will use closing price and the period default (most commonly used value) is 50, which makes the moving average sensitive to prices over the past 50 periods while for a swing trader you'd be interested in days.

Benefits of Moving Averages

In technical analysis, moving averages are going to help you look at two important things. The first is they help identify trends. In a minute we'll see how you can do that. Second, they help you identify support and resistance levels. They do this far better than what you can do by simply drawing straight lines on your charts, even though we spent a lot of time doing that in the last chapter.

Exponential moving averages

You can also generate exponential moving averages. An exponential moving average has a really complicated formula, so we aren't going to work through that part, you can simply use any stock website to add an exponential moving average to a chart. The important thing to remember about exponential moving averages is that they are more sensitive to recent prices. The reason is that the exponential moving average uses weighting that gives more recent prices more emphasis. That makes more sense, especially when you are a swing trader and more interested in shorter-term price changes. With a simple moving average, a price from two months ago has the same weight as yesterday's price, and that might not be relevant to you.

Breaks above and below the long term MA

Typically, 50-day and 200-day moving averages are used in charts. What you're looking for are movements of the short term moving average above and below the longer term moving average. That can indicate a change in trend.

You can see this kind of movement in the chart below, which shows SPY over a one year period. The purple line is a 50-day simple moving average, and the green line is the 200-day moving average. So we are looking for points at which the purple line, or shorter term moving average, crosses above or below the longer term moving average (the green line).

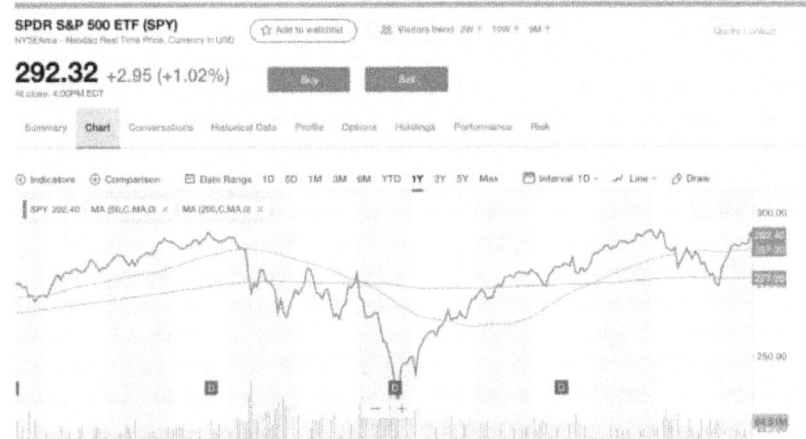

You can clearly see that the purple line went below the green line before there was a major decline in the share price. So had you been paying attention, you might have been able to take advantage of the situation either by shorting the stock or perhaps by investing in some put options.

Later, you will also notice that the short term MA crossed back above the longer term MA, perhaps indicating an uptrend. The dip you see in the chart is actually a short term market decline that happened as a result of some tweets from President Trump, so it may not have any real significance related to the longer term trends.

The data provided by a moving average isn't perfect, but you can use moving averages to estimate support and resistance levels. In an upward trend, a 50-day moving average will give you the support level for the data. So it can be used to estimate what you should use for your stop-loss price. The position of the current price relative to the 50-day moving average will give you an indication of trend. In our examples, we are looking at past behavior, but you are going to want to look more at current behavior when trying to determine when to enter or exit trades. In the chart for Apple below, notice the position of the handles relative to the purple line, which gives the 50-day moving average.

When the trend is up, the candles are above the 50-day moving average. Then when the trend is down, notice that the candles are below the 50-day moving average. This can help you estimate what the current trend is. You should combine your estimate using this technique with data from other indicators.

Buy signals

When a short term moving average crosses above a longer-term moving average that can be taken as a buy signal if you are hoping for a rising share price. Notice in this chart for Apple, the 10-day moving average has recently crossed above the 50 days moving average, possibly signaling a coming uptrend.

You can also observe from the chart that when the short term moving average crosses below the long term moving average, you see a sell signal. Indeed, that played out with a declining share price.

Exponential versus Simple Moving Averages

As we said earlier, an exponential moving average is more sensitive to recent prices. Since an exponential moving average is more sensitive to recent prices, it might be able to give us faster insight into coming trend changes. That is, it will detect a trend change before a simple moving average. However, keep in mind that a lot of short term fluctuations in share price are simply due to noise or random behavior. That means that an exponential moving average might give more weight to meaningless price fluctuations than it should.

In any case, a rising exponential moving average can be taken to indicate a rising share price and vice versa. A good buy signal with the exponential moving average is to look for a rising exponential moving average but with share prices below it. If the exponential moving average is declining, and the stock price dips below it that might mean its time to sell your shares.

This is noticeable in the chart below, which shows a 50-day exponential moving average. Notice that soon after share prices drop below the moving average, there is a dip in stock prices. This was a solid sell signal in the data, had you been paying attention (or a signal to short). You can also see in this upward trend, the share prices remaining above the exponential average are a solid buy signal.

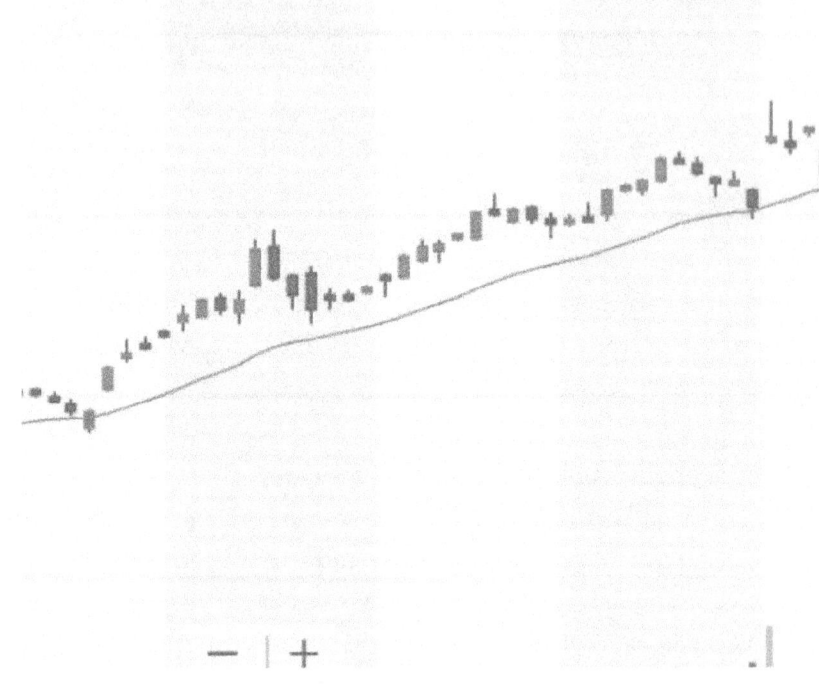

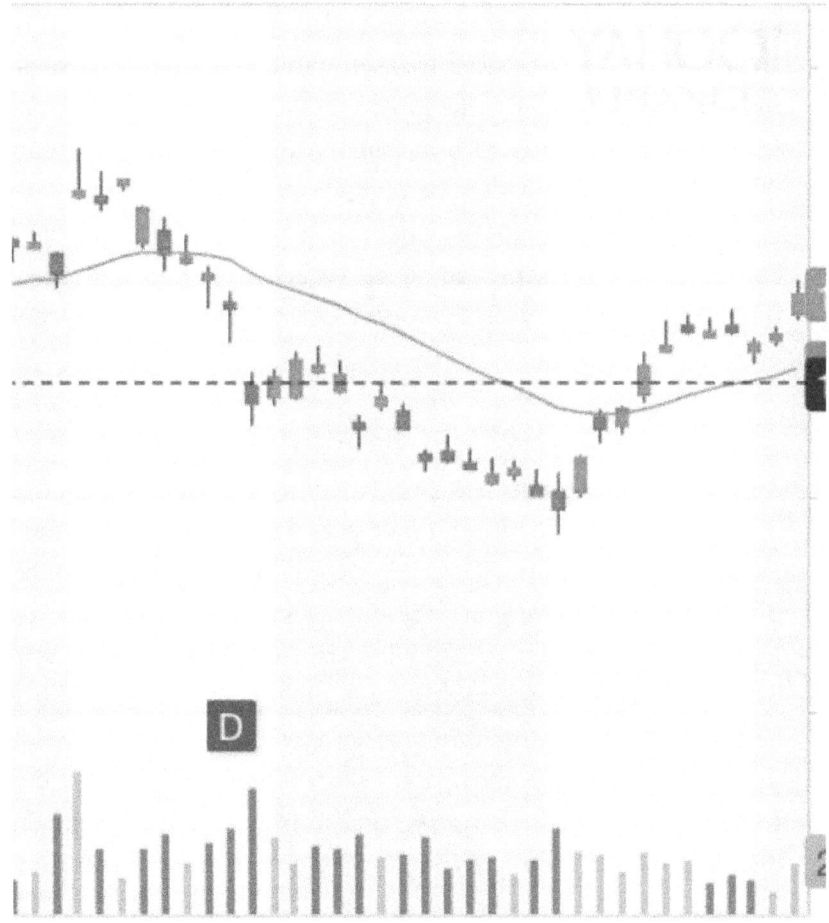

You can also relate exponential moving averages to zones of support and resistance. A downward trending moving average can indicate resistance. If it is upward trending, that can indicate a level of support.

Time Periods

Remember that as a swing trader, you are more interested in longer-term time horizons than a day trader. Maybe you may not be as interested in the type of price weighting that an exponential moving average gives you, but that depends. Swing trading can run from a couple of days out to months. If you are more interested in shorter time frames, then you might prefer looking at exponential moving averages, while if you are interested in months of time for your trades, simple moving averages might work better for you.

Generally speaking, a 20-day moving average can be used to seek out indications of trends. You can also use a 50-day moving average for this purpose. To spot levels of support and resistance, a 100-day moving average is preferred.

Special trading signals

When different period moving averages cross each other, in particular when a shorter period moving average crosses above or below a longer period moving average on the same chart, this can be an important trading signal. A golden cross occurs when a short term moving average crosses above the longer-term moving average. This can be taken as a strong indication of an upward trend in price. When the opposite move occurs, that is a short term moving average crosses below a long term moving average. This is called a "death cross," meaning that the coming pricing trend is expected to be down.

Bollinger Bands

If you want to identify levels of support and resistance in a stock chart and do it in as close to real time as possible, Bollinger Bands may be the tool that you should be using. Using Bollinger bands, you can find out price levels that stocks are unlikely to break above or fall below in the near future. This can help you figure out exit points (i.e., the selling price you should be willing to accept on trade) and stop-loss orders (the low price you are willing to absorb as a loss).

Bollinger bands are called "bands" because they will show you the two zones of resistance and support simultaneously. You will see the share price fluctuating inside the two bands. This gives us a measure of volatility, but the most important thing about Bollinger bands is that the data they provide is dynamic, that is changing with time. The width of the bands is a measure of the stocks volatility or the magnitude of price swings. Bollinger bands actually include three curves. In the middle, you'll see a moving average.

Since volatility is measured in standard deviations, when you add Bollinger bands, it is going to ask you how many standard deviations you want to use on the chart, along with a period to specify for your moving average. The defaults are 2 standard deviations and a 20-period moving average. Although sometimes you are going to see stock prices go outside the Bollinger bands, for the most part, they stay inside. Here is a chart showing Apple with Bollinger bands over a six month time period:

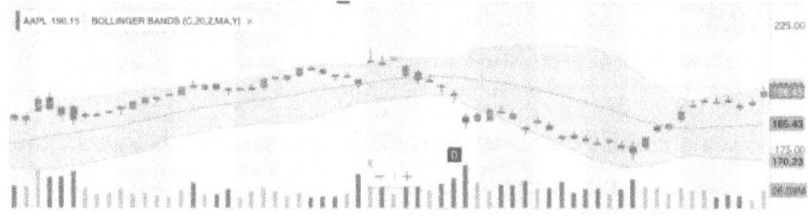

The wider the bands, the more volatility there is in the stock. If the bands are narrow, that indicates low volatility. We will see that Telsa has very little volatility, this is indicated in this chart, and the Bollinger bands are narrow.

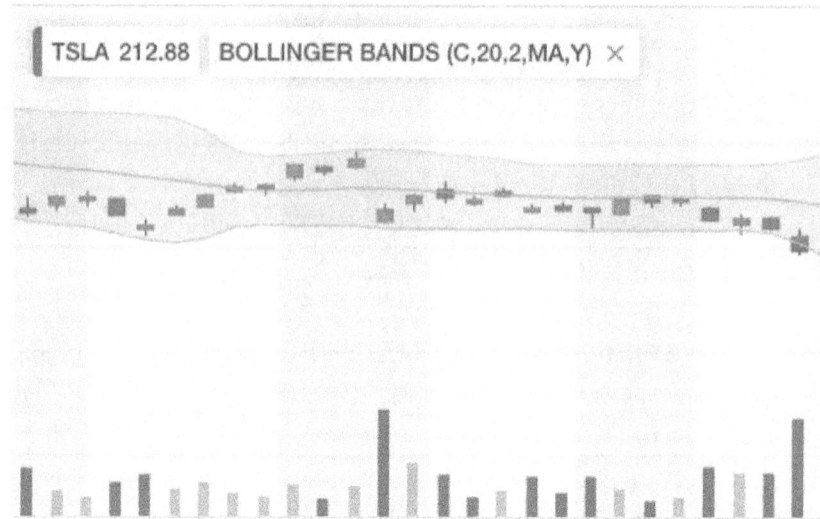

Compare that to the Apple chart, which shows wider Bollinger bands. Apple has much higher volatility than Tesla does.

Bollinger bands also serve other purposes. For example, one thing that traders are interested in is whether or not a given stock is overpriced (at a premium), just right, or low priced (discount). When stock prices are above the moving average, they can be considered to be at a premium that is overpriced. When they drop below the moving average, they are underpriced, so at a discount. They are considered just right when they are at the moving average.

Another thing that traders look at when considering Bollinger bands is whether or not a stock is overbought or oversold. An overbought stock is one set for price declines. To see this in a Bollinger band, look for the wicks of the candlesticks to touch or go outside the upper limit of the Bollinger bands, and expect a price drop thereafter.

An oversold stock can be expected to start trending upward in price. In that case, you want to look for candlestick wicks to touch the lower Bollinger band, or even fall outside of it.

When the body of a candlestick falls completely outside of a Bollinger band, this is taken to be a reversal signal. Two reversal signals are clearly apparent in this chart of SNAP. Two candlesticks whose bodies fell outside the Bollinger bands are noted, and the following trend reversals are apparent.

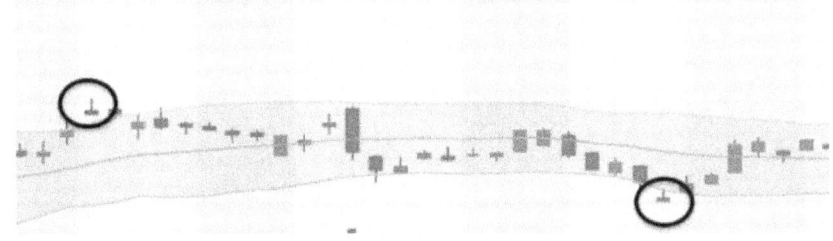

The RSI

The RSI or relative strength index is a measure that sets up boundary values for stock that can indicate overbought or oversold shares. The RSI is a type of oscillator. It can help you determine the momentum a given stock has, giving an estimate of the speed of price movements. If the RSI goes above 70, this is an indication that the stock is overbought. When you see an RSI above 70, that means that a downward trend or price reversal may be coming. If it falls below 30, that indicates the stock is oversold, and an upward trend may be coming.

MACD

MACD means moving average convergence divergence. This fancy title means that you generate an indicator that subtracts the 26-day moving average from the 12-day moving average. That is called the MACD line. A 9-day exponential moving average is also shown, which is the "signal line." If the MACD crosses above the signal line, traders take this as a buy signal. If it does below, that is taken as a sell signal. In the chart below, the orange line is the signal, and the purple line is the MACD line. Notice that the purple line crosses above the signal line, so it's a buy. In fact, on the stock chart above, there was an upward trend after the crossing.

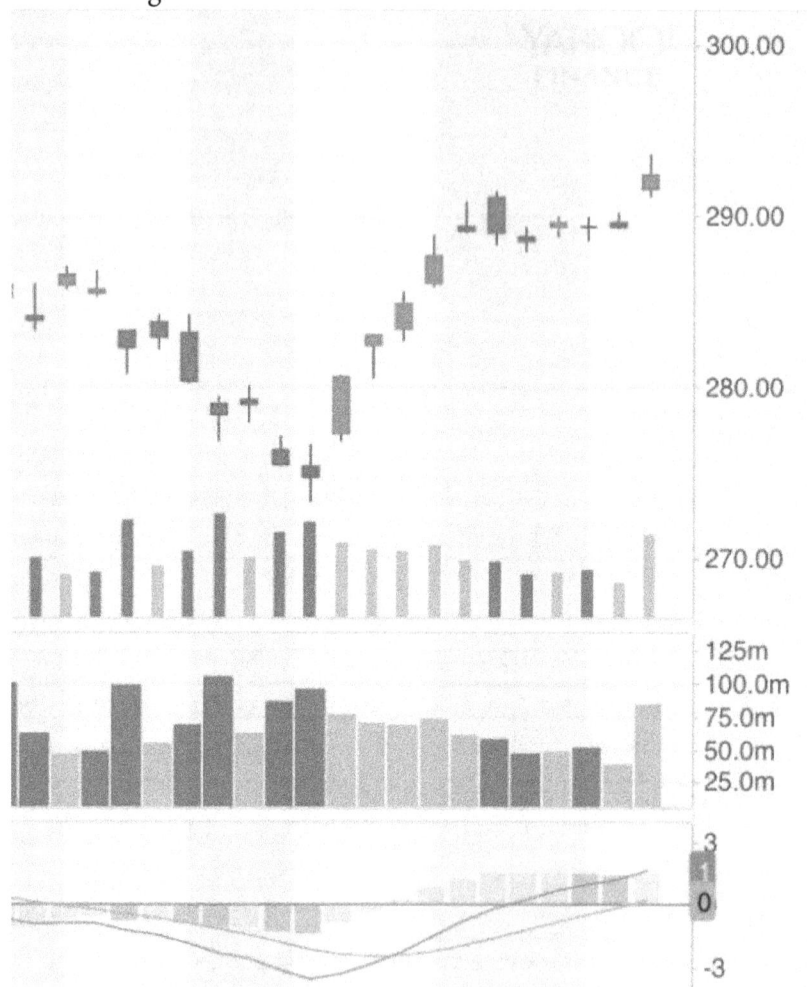

Directional Movement Index

Next, we consider the directional movement index or DMI. This is important because it gives you a measure of the strength of trends, for example, how well did bullish investors do in pushing up the price, or bearish investors do at pushing down the price. These are measured in two trends +DMI and -DMI. The difference between these two trends is called the ADX. On most charts, all three will be shown on the same graph.

Crossovers of +DMI and -DMI are indicators of whether or not bearish investors or bullish investors have stronger momentum. In the chart below, the +DMI line is green, and the –DMI line is red. A point where the +DMI line has crossed below the –DMI line is noted. That would indicate a sell signal, and looking up the dashed line to the stock chart, you see that the share price did decline to a minimum.

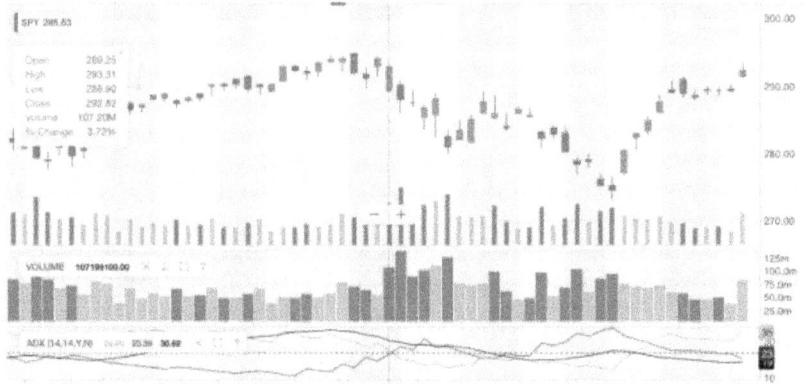

Notice toward the right that there is a point where the +DMI (green line) crossed above the –DMI line (red), indicating that bullish investors had their way. This is born out in the chart where there is a strong upward trend in price after the crossing.

The Hull Moving Average

The Hull moving average was developed to eliminate some of the weaknesses of other moving averages. It seeks to reduce the lagging effect that comes with a moving average more efficiently than an exponential moving average (which used weighting for the same purpose). Typically a 20 or 50-period Hull moving average is used. It fits stock data to a very accurate degree, and traders look for turns in the curve line to indicate buying and selling signals.

In the chart below, we see a 20-period Hull moving average overlaid on SPY. Notice how nicely it fits the actual pricing data. We have annotated the chart with black arrows that indicate turning points in the curve. When the Hull moving average turns upward, that is an indication of a buy signal. When it turns downward, that is a sell signal. The high accuracy of the Hull moving average is quite impressive, and it seems like a solid indicator to use.

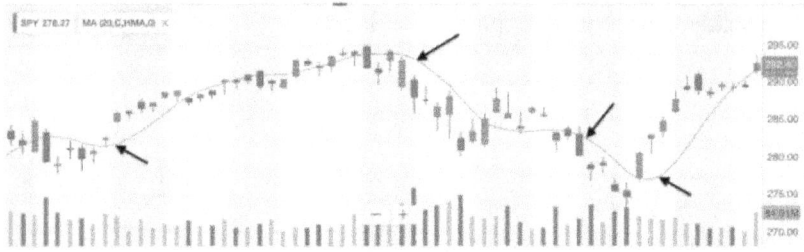

Like other moving averages, you can use short-term, and longer-term Hull moving averages and look for crossover points to get a more accurate indication of a buy or sell signal. The principles used here are the same as those used with other moving averages, so when the short term Hull moving average crosses above a longer-term Hull moving average, that is a buy signal. On the other hand, when a short term Hull moving average crosses below a longer-term Hull moving average that can be taken to be a sell signal.

Flags

The next thing we are going to look for is patterns in stock charts that show sudden movement up or down. These are called flags. The analogy here is that the "flagpole" indicates a sharp rise in price over a short time period, while the "flag" can be a zone of stable prices within a narrow range. The chart may look something like this:

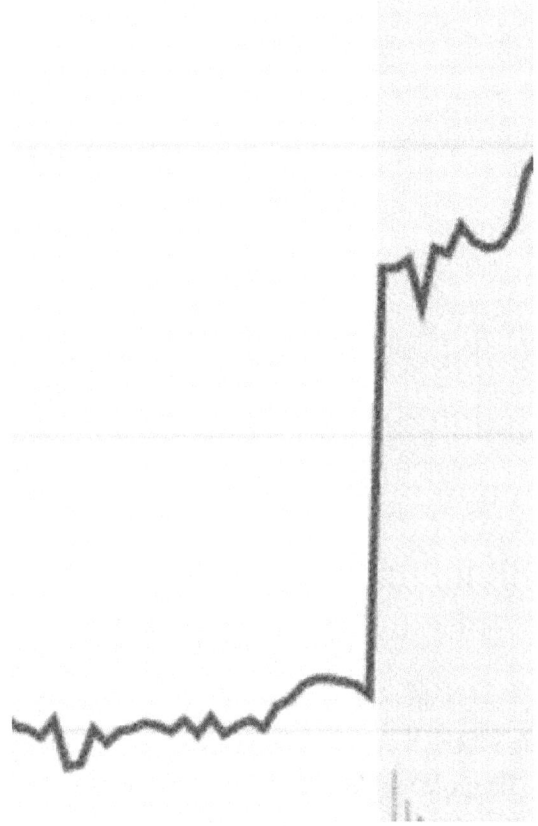

Since the flag, in this case, shot upwards, this is a bull flag. To be a true flag, we need more than just the pattern, you want to check the volume of trading as well. If there is high volume, then the flag can be a signal of further price increases. On the other hand, the price may remain trapped or boxed in at the top of the flagpole, and only fluctuate a bit for a time within the box. In the example above, the stock is SNAP. The volume in the lower area was quite muted, with daily volume ranging between 122k-134k. Entering the bottom of the flagpole, volume shot up to 719k. At the top of the flag pole, it shot up again, to 1.6 M. The large increases in volume are indicative that this is a solid opportunity and a real bull flag. In fact, carrying it out a few days later, we see more increases in share price:

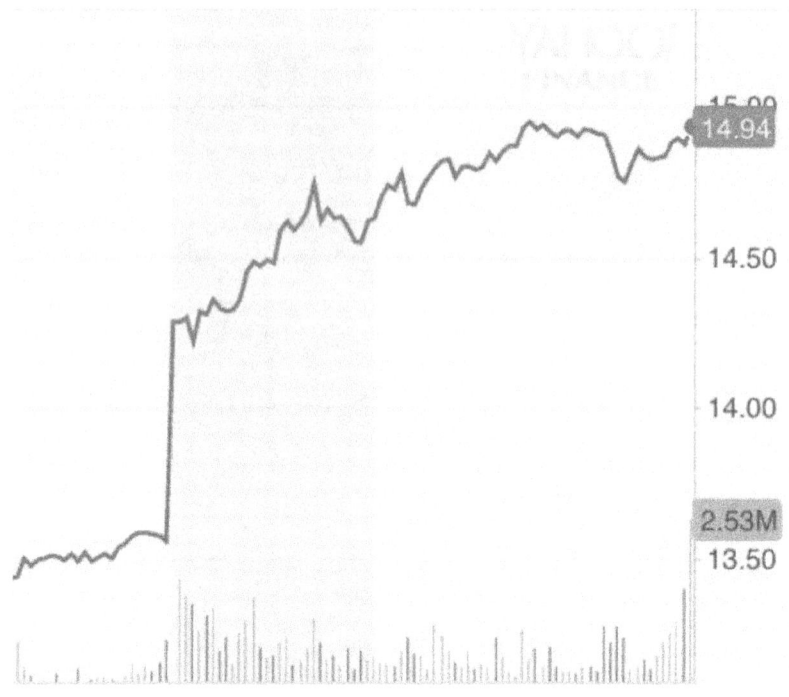

As you can see from the bars at the bottom of the chart, the volume remains strong all the way to the right-hand side. Entering a trade at the top of the flagpole would have been a reasonable move for a swing trader. To have a successful trade, you can put a stop loss order of 1% risk below the top of the flag pole. You have to be prepared for the situation where the top of the flag is going to be a resistance, rather than a true breakout. In this case, it's a true rise in the share price. Always pay attention to volume.

Of course, flag patterns can be inverted and work for suddenly declining prices as well. In that case, it's a bear flag. Again, knowing whether or not it's a true flag can hinge on volume. Always compare the volume to see if traders are flocking to the stock or selling it off. Low volume indicates that there isn't much interest in the stock as far as buying and selling right now, and so the price move may not be significant and you might be witnessing a move to support or resistance instead.

So if a flag is real, where does this come from? More than likely, it comes from a significant announcement by the company or a surprising earnings call. That is, the company may have had an earnings report that beat expectations. We discuss these items in the chapter on fundamentals, and if you are a good trader, you are paying attention to fundamentals and not just technical indicators. That means that you would know this might be coming or be ready to act on it before anyone else (anyone else, among individual investors), instead of staring at charts looking for mysterious patterns. Of course, we aren't saying to use the technical analysis or look for patterns like this in the charts – but rather that you should do both and sometimes take your nose out of the trees. That means paying attention to financial and business news and reading about the companies you are interested in trading.

How many indicators can you use?

There are many indicators – maybe even too many. Looking at all of them will make your head spin. Are you supposed to use all of them?

In fact, we haven't even covered all of them. I invite the reader to open up a stock chart on Yahoo Finance or their favorite trading website and explore all the possible indicators they can add onto their charts.

The reality is at some point, you are not going to be getting any additional information from paying attention to more and more indicators. You are going to have to settle on a small number of indicators and accept the results that come from that.

First off, every trader should use basic chart reading. That is a common sense level of analysis, but it is still important. It's the starting point of any analysis, but shouldn't be your final guide to making a decision to enter a trade or not.

Second, candlesticks are time tested and proven method. But remember that candlesticks are not fool proof, they only serve as a guide. But it's a solid guide to include in your analysis. It's hard to find a trader – any trader – who is not using candlesticks. You should take your time to study them well beyond the introductory information that we've provided in this book.

So we are at a point where you should use candlesticks and eyeball charts for levels of support and resistance. What about all the others? Certainly using moving averages is useful, but you shouldn't get caught up in picking which moving averages to use. They all have merits and drawbacks. I have found the Hull moving average to be pretty exceptional.

Bollinger bands are also useful, especially as an aid in determining the levels of support and resistance.

The bottom line is that adding more and more indicators is not going to give you more information in the end. Many of the different indicators are different flavors of the same information. So settling on one of the other might even be said to come down to a matter of personal taste.

It's also better to thoroughly understand and use 1-2 indicators than it is to have a shallow use of 10 different indicators. Our personal preference is to use candlesticks, Bollinger bands, and Hull moving averages, and we don't even always use Bollinger bands. But we are not here to tell you which ones to use, you can use this book as a guide for introducing you to the world of indicators, and then study them in detail elsewhere and make the choices that fit you the best. You might also end up changing things as time moves on, trying different indicators, and finding out that others work better for you.

Remember that there is no magic tool that is going to guarantee riches. The indicators are there to help you make your trades, but they cannot tell you what trades to make. In the end, the best indicator is the one between your ears, and you will have to be the one that does the analysis and makes the decisions. Not all decisions are going to be the right ones, and even experienced traders make bad trades, so when it gets down to it don't blame the indicators, some trades are just not going to work out.

Chapter 8: Deadly Trading Mistakes

Coming up next is a list of nine things you need to maintain a strategic distance from no matter what. Anybody of them can pulverize your monetary dreams and objectives!

1. Trading with money you can't bear to lose.

One of the best obstructions to active trading is utilizing the money that you indeed can't bear to lose. Instances of this would be money that should be used to pay the home loan, bills or your tyke's school educational cost. This is sometimes alluded to as "trading with frightened money," and there is an excellent purpose behind that. Eventually what happens is that when somebody knows in the back of their mind that they are risking the lease money, they trade out of dread and emotion versus rationale and no emotion. On the off chance that you are in this circumstance, I exceedingly suggest that you quit trading until you earn enough to put into an account that you genuinely can stand to lose without causing major budgetary mishaps. You can begin with as meager as $2000 and trade stocks under $30.

2. They should be "certain."

We as a whole want to ensure that the trade we need to make will be a decent one. Along these lines, we search for signs that will give us an affirmation to enter. This can come in a few structures, for instance... Tuning into CNBC or the Wall Street Journal to provide us with news that our stock is progressing or hanging tight for two or three additional days to ensure that the stock is genuinely flying and only not on a false breakout. Different traders will get sentiments from companions, family or broker. Others will trust that ten technical indicators will arrange and give the "green light."

These are all right to a point, anyway the enormous mistake to stay away from is taking so much time that you let the trade take off without you. Curiously, what winds up occurring because of holding up too long is that you increment your risk. This is because as the stock moves ever more elevated there are fewer buyers left in the market, and it can come tumbling down until more buyer's venture in. It resembles a round of a game of seat juggling; in the end, somebody gets captured without a seat. Traders who pause and pause and hang tight to ensure are typically the ones buying the top tick just before the stocks sells off. They at that point beat themselves up supposing they picked the wrong stock. Chances are it had nothing to do with their choice, simply poor planning. The thing to remember is that there can be no total sureness in some random trade. All we ever can do is go out on a limb along with an act of pure trust!

3. Spending profits before you make them.

Nothing is all the more energizing at that point getting into a trade that takes off and places you into an exceedingly favorable circumstance. This can cause severe issues in any case, since this sort of trade places you in an exceedingly euphoric state and prompts daydreaming about the huge profits still to come. You state "Wow I'm now up 15% in two days; I'll be up half in a week and likely twofold my money in no time!" Then the following thing that happens is you are settling on the extraordinary new vehicle you are going to buy or maybe telling your supervisor that he can stick it... Well, you get the thought! The genuine issue happens as you become involved with the daydream and desires. This makes you not be set up to get out as the market sells off and gobbles up your profits since you have persuaded yourself regarding the possible result and will preclude the truth from claiming the circumstance. The straightforward solution for this is to know where and how you will take profits once you enter the trade. Additionally, understand that the market will go up as long as it needs and not how high you figure it ought to go.

4. Shaping a feeling.

I'm here to reveal to you that the market does not care at all about you or your sentiments. Regardless of whether they depend on meticulous research or from a "Money Street Guru," it doesn't make a difference!

Possibly your assessment on market direction for the long term is right. However, it doesn't imply that in the short-term things can't move against you. Keep in mind that there are a huge number of traders out there who likewise have a conclusion. It is all these distinctive sentiments that can cause incredible variances in cost on some random day or week paying little heed to your viewpoint

5. Three 4-letter words that will murder you! Expectation - WISH - PRAY

If you ever end up completing at least one of the above mentioned while in a trade then you are stuck in an unfortunate situation! As I have just stated, the market doesn't care at all. All the trusting, wishing and imploring on the planet won't turn a losing trade into a triumphant one. When you are incorrect, utilize a straightforward 4-letter word to address the circumstance SELL!

6. Not adhering to your plan.

A primary wellspring of inconvenience arises when a trader begins to go astray from their strategy. Possibly for seven days, they will trade as per one lot of principles and the following use something extraordinary.

This flying by the seat of the jeans dependably winds up exploded backward. This is because the trader can never be sure what is working and what is most certainly not. You should never go amiss from your system once you begin. For whatever length of time that it is a decent one statistically, there is positively no motivation to transform it. The best approach to profit from it is to trade it again and again to abuse the edge it gives you.

One thing to likewise know about is that a trader is most powerless against exchanging approaches after a couple of losses. In this way, give uncommon consideration at these times.

7. Not realizing how to escape a losing trade.

Buy As I continue saying the market does not mind what you think. It does what it does, and when you are incorrect you are incorrect! The least demanding approach to shield an awful trade from going downright terrible is to determine before you get in, where you will get out. You can utilize a dollar sum or at some objective point, for example, the low of the past 15-minute bar. Make beyond any doubt you don't get the "dazed deer in the headlights disorder". This is the place you see the stock tumble to your stop loss indicates. However, you are unfit to make a move. Perhaps this is because of dread or disbelief that you are incorrect, yet except if you get out ASAP you could finish up I major budgetary inconvenience!

8. Having a sense of self.

I have seen various people enter the trading diversion that was incredibly fruitful in different business adventures. Given this, they had a genuinely substantial inner self and figured they couldn't fall flat. Their self-images turned into their defeat since they couldn't deal except that they weren't right and would not ransom of awful trades. Indeed, whoever or wherever you originated from does not concern the markets. All the appeal, forces of influence, number of confirmations on the divider or business insightful won't move the market when you are incorrect.

9. Going gaga for a stock or trade.

Give me a chance to give you a case of what I mean. Back in the spring of 1999 EFAX was a boiling stock. I held on to buy it on a plunge and did as such at $19/share. It began to climb certainly, and life was incredible! Sooner or later, however, it began to return to my entry point and afterward beneath it. Here's the issue. For reasons unknown I truly loved EFAX and ended up connected to it. Eventually,

I couldn't relinquish it even though I realized I should. I defended and legitimized why my dear companion should skip back. However, it never did. I at long last needed to sever my relationship when the stock hit $9.

MARKET AND TRADING PSYCHOLOGY

Everybody that trades totally should assess their trading brain research frequently. A large number of us have found out about the impacts of fear and greed we experience when we trade the markets. What's more, more than likely, you have pondered internally "I'm not fearful" and "I'm not greedy". The truth is "Truly, you are". We each experience distinctive dimensions of fear and greed in a trade. When we state 'fear,' we are not discussing you are squatting in a fetal position in the corner trembling and influencing forward and backward. What's more, when we state 'greed' we are not discussing you are tweaking your hands, salivating at the mouth like you would envision Mr. Tightwad. Fear and greed are unpretentious in a trade and can interchange forward and backward from one another inside seconds.

Fear:

At the point when the market quickly moves against our trade, you may see a prompt rise in your nervousness. Prepared traders are utilized to this since it is very occasional that a trader will wind up in a real predicament or top of any trade to make an entry. Oft it isn't that feeling you get when somebody hops out and alarms you. It isn't that feeling like nearly getting hit by a vehicle. Nor is it the inclination that you have when viewing a terrifying motion picture. More often than not, fear in the market is a subtler encounter. You will have a hard time remembering it as fear necessarily because your mind will be gotten up to speed at the time. You will be caught up with attempting to settle on a significant decision and discerning the future remorseful distastefulness you will understand whether the wrong choice is made. After a decision is made and you are finished celebrating your most recent triumph or lamenting the disappointment of your choice, venture back and give yourself a legitimate, non-stooping, non-self-indulging analysis. You will find that fear had gone into the condition of a proper conclusion. Continuously know about this emotion. You have never given it a chance to choose your destiny. The best way to overcome it is to plan and adhere to that plan. Plan your entry, your leave, your target(s). Make a point to have elective procedures if there should arise an occurrence of various situations that could become possibly the most important factor with your trade. In finding out about fear and greed in the market, I have seen that something was missing in those works. Patience is never referenced. Patience can amplify fear and greed. Since we are discussing fear, we should take a gander at how patience impacts fear inside the trade. Situation:

Your trade is moving against you. You are losing money. You feel that unfilled premonition and slight frenzy. On the off chance that you give the situation a lot of patience, you could be in for more profound losses. On the off chance that you have too little patience, you could leave the trade rashly and miss out on much-invited additions. So, what do you do? Now in the diversion, it is a hurl up. Try not to whip yourself too severely on the off chance that you settle on the wrong decision yet ensure you learn from this experience. The exercise in learning is to plan BEFORE you click that catch that gets you into the trade in any case. Many prepared traders fall into the snare of neglecting to plan correctly as well. They get arrogant, yet the market will tell them soon enough of their failings.

Exercises Learned [hopefully before you place a trade]:

Fear is continuously present in a business. Try not to give it a chance to control you. Patience intensifies fearful sentiments.

Plan your trade.

Trading ought to exhaust. On the off chance that you need the enthusiasm and rush of the rollercoaster ride of 'money related emotion,' go betting. If you need to prevail as a trader, plan your trade and trade your plan - keep it exhausting. Just trade what you can bear to lose.

Make sure beyond a shadow of a doubt that the money you use to trade is intellectual, disposable capital. If you wind up in an 'unquestionable requirement win' trade, your decision-production capacities will be incredibly frustrated. This, along with patience, will intensify your sentiments of fear and greed.

Greed:

You make an incredible entry. You have perused to give the great sections a chance to ride while you cut the terrible passages off. Greed is a piece of amusement. You need to ensure that you snatch all that you can because the following trade may make you lose more than you would hope to lose. You would prefer not to leave any money on the table - people, this is greed. Greed can turn into fear all around rapidly. Greed, similar to fear, is additionally an inconspicuous emotion with regards to trading the markets. It is likely subtler than fear. Nobody likes to consider themselves being greedy. Furthermore, it is presumably evident that you are not greedy at everything except rather greed can assume a ground-breaking job in your trades. It won't resemble the greed of Mr. Penny pincher. Sweat-soaked palms, a little spot of slobber and a somewhat stern face will likely not be on your trades' motivation. More probable, without a plan, you will hold tight to trade excessively long or hop in at the wrong minute to satisfy your dream of profiting. Trading, in itself, verifies that fear and greed exists. This is basically because you will need to stop your losses while giving your additions a chance to keep running the extent that they can. This gives fertile ground to greed and fear to develop.

When greed has dominated, and you commit your error, greed can turn to fear in all respects rapidly. A stock trader can encounter fear and greed a few times inside one trading day. I have by and by having had greed turn to fear at that point back to greed again inside seconds. Try not to ride this sloping ride. Make sure to do your best to dispose of the emotion by planning.

The more emotional you become, the more probable you are to commit an error. We should take this unusual to make a point. Specialists are not permitted (by and large) to perform a medical procedure on a friend or family member. Relatives and dear companions must look for assistance from another specialist. Why? The specialist is emotionally included, connected to the patient. That is an issue since emotion fits committing errors. The equivalent is valid for trading the markets. Where does patience become possibly the most crucial factor with greed? Patience collaborates with. Similarly, it does with fear. It enhances the emotion. If you have a lot of patience with trade and become greedy, you can lose a considerable segment of your increases if not finish up with a loss on a trade that was performing incredibly. You should leave when your plan directs that you exit. You could likewise go into a trade rashly. A trade you ought to have avoided in any case. The accompanying should look extremely well-known to you from the Fear data. Continuously know about this emotion. You have never given it a chance to choose your destiny.

The best way to defeat it is to plan and adhere to that plan. Plan your entry, your leave, your target(s). Make a point to have elective procedures if there should be an occurrence of various situations that could become possibly the most important factor with your trade. Patience can amplify fear and greed. Exercises Learned [hopefully before you place a trade]:

Greed is continuously present in a trade. Try not to give it a chance to control you. Patience intensifies greedy emotions. Plan your trade. [Echo, Echo] Plan your trade. Trading ought to exhaust. If you need the fervor and rush of the rollercoaster ride of 'budgetary emotion', go betting. On the off chance that you need to prevail as a trader, plan your trade and trade your plan - keep it exhausting. Just trade what you can stand to lose. Make sure beyond a shadow of a doubt that the money you use to trade is intellectual, disposable capital. On the off chance that you wind up in an 'unquestionable requirement win' trade, your decision-production capacities will be extraordinarily impeded. This, along with patience, will intensify your sentiments of fear and greed.

Patience:

Something you most likely haven't found out about is how patience influences fear and greed. I imagine this is an essential piece of fear and greed that nobody ever discusses. Basically, "Patience enhances fear and greed." The absence of patients may make you enter or leave a trade that you ought to have avoided in any case. The excess of patience may make you exit, enter or remain in a trade that you ought to have left.

Conclusion

Congratulations on making it this far! You deserve some applause because this is a very dense book and its true value is apparent only upon repeated reading. The main cause for this is new traders entering the markets with the wrong expectations.

Everyone who wishes to trade wants to have a lot of money. This is perfectly fine. However, very few are willing to put in the work necessary. If you want an easy way to make money, trading is not it! You're better off engaging in something else. Trading successfully is a skill that takes a lot of time and patience.

Not only do you have to master your strategy, you must, crucially, master yourself. You need to know yourself inside and out if you are to succeed in this endeavor. You need to put in a lot of work examining your beliefs about money, success and what it is you want in life. Remember, if there's a block in any of this, you will not be successful in trading no matter how good your technical skill is.

Take the time to practice first then get on a demo platform and only when you consistently make money on demo, go live. Many traders get impatient with this process and push forward as fast as possible. The specter of time is one of the biggest reasons for this. Most people reason that they need to become successful traders in the shortest time possible or they want to be like that other trader who became a millionaire within a year and so on.

Letting go of time limits is one of the first things you need to do. Simply accept it will take however long it has to take and you will eventually get there. Think of it this way. If you need to get to another town for an important engagement, will you worry about how long it takes to get there? Beyond the initial planning phase, probably not. You'll simply travel to the place and during your journey, you simply deal with whatever comes. You don't sit there wishing you get there a day earlier or an hour earlier etc. You might wish for it but it isn't your overriding concern. You just accept that you arrive whenever it is you arrive.

Treat trading in the same manner and stick to the path prescribed in this book. As your skill progresses, you will find suitable tasks to take on to enhance and satisfy your new skill level. Above all else, maintain a balanced, calm mindset and let it guide you forward.

Wishing you the best of luck in this endeavor! Hopefully, your thinking has been challenged and changed after reading this book. If you feel it was of some use to you, please do leave a review, it will be greatly appreciated!

Don't miss out!

Visit the website below and you can sign up to receive emails whenever Michael Branson publishes a new book. There's no charge and no obligation.

https://books2read.com/r/B-A-MWSI-YCJAB

BOOKS 2 READ

Connecting independent readers to independent writers.

Did you love *Swing Trading A Beginners And Advanced Guide For Effective Trading Tactics, Make More Money And Reach Financial Freedom*? Then you should read *Forex Trading + Money Management Strategies For Beginners 2 books in 1 Learn Trading Psychology, Trading Tactics, Become Debt Free And Create Passive Income* by Leonardo Turner!

Forex Trading + Money Management Strategies For Beginners 2 books in 1

In this book, you will learn all the basic information you need to start understanding foreign exchange currencies, and how to trade them. You will learn exactly what Forex is, and why you should dabble in the art of trading it.

You will learn about the risk vs. the reward, and much much more. All lined out with clear and concise instructions, tips, and other indicators to make this book simple and enjoyable to read.

I hope you find what you need, and that this book is what gives you the push to start this fun adventure in the currency trading world.

One of the most important steps towards being independent is financial independence. This means you are in total control of your expenses and the money you make.

Money is crucial when it comes to living well in the community, but you don't need too much money to become independent, happy, or even successful. You merely need to know how to control your expenses and manage the money you have so that it can work for you.

Debts can be a source of worry and anxiety for many people, and sometimes, it can be tough to know where to start when you want to manage your financial debts. This book will help you to get started on the path to paying off all your debts and become debt free. The book will provide you with a clear picture of how much money you owe, and to whom, how you can contact credit card companies and negotiate interest rates, how you can prioritize which debt to pay off first, which strategy to adopt to clear your debts, and how to create a budget. Also, the book is meant to teach you the most important aspects of personal finance.

Besides that, you will further learn how to get started with investments and make sure that your money works for you, and not the other way around. You will be taken through many exciting tips and lessons that you should follow to fulfill your financial goals.

Also by Michael Branson

Swing Trading A Beginners And Advanced Guide For Effective Trading Tactics, Make More Money And Reach Financial Freedom

CPSIA information can be obtained
at www.ICGtesting.com
Printed in the USA
BVHW071932110819
555624BV00001B/200/P